Remember When...

A nostalgic view of the cultural heritage of Elberton, Georgia

By

CAROLYN J. BOND

God Bless!
Carolyn J. Bond

Copyright © 2019 Carolyn J. Bond

ISBN 978-0-359-97732-1

All rights reserved. No part of this book may be reproduced or used in any manner without written permission of Carolyn J. Bond except for the use of quotations in a book review.

Independently Published by Carolyn J. Bond
1143 Athens Hwy.
Elberton, Georgia USA 30635

First Edition August 2019

Cover photo By Rachel D. White *my granddaughter*
Cover design By Charles Prier

Editing and Publishing Services
By Charles Prier

Know-It-All Publications
1481 Lankford Road
Bowersville, Georgia USA 30516
www.KiaPublications.com

Dedication

To every Elbertonian
who has commented
with pleasure on the articles

Acknowledgements

To my husband Cecil, who drove me around town, found New Street for me, and aided my memory of many places and events.

Preface

I have always been interested in the history of Elbert County and have a selection of historical/genealogical books from which I drew thoughts. Because of the many requests I've received since 1913, which was the beginning of printing in The Elberton Star, I followed through by placing all the articles together in a book.

Table of Contents

Chapter 1 About the Author	8
Chapter 2 Elbert County	11
Chapter 3 The Elberton Square	19
Chapter 4 Around the Square	27
Chapter 5 North McIntosh Street aka One Way Street	41
Chapter 6 Elbert Street Right Side from North Oliver..	47
Chapter 7 Heard Street from Square	55
Chapter 8 Car Dealerships in Elberton	63
Chapter 9 Elberton's Service Stations	67
Chapter 10 Old-Time Businesses	73
Chapter 11 Colorful Places and Events	79
Chapter 12 Elberton's Mills	87
Chapter 13 Seaboard Airline Traveling Library	95
Chapter 14 Good Eating	101
Chapter 15 Elberton's Barber Shops	103
Chapter 16 Pitts Pool	109
Chapter 17 The Elberton Brickyard	111
Chapter 18 Jack and Jill Kindergarten	115
Chapter 19 The Burning of Central School	119
Chapter 20 Snuggling Birds	127
Chapter 21 Nancy and I	129
Chapter 22 Birds and Snakes	135

Chapter 23 Johnson Life	139
Chapter 24 Cleveland Family Furniture	145
Chapter 25 Flying South	149
Chapter 26 Christmas 1952	153
Chapter 27 Christmas Poem	157
Chapter 28 Hummingbirds	159
Chapter 29 Little Red Wagon	161

Chapter 1
About the Author

My name is Carolyn J. Bond. I am a lifelong resident of Elberton, Georgia. This book comes from information gained through my life experiences, reading, talking with friends, relatives and others who lived during the same era, and research for writing "Remember When" and other articles published in "The Elberton Star."

As I write this book I am confronted with the troubling reality that everything won't be presented exactly as each reader may remember. I can assure you that I have been diligent in seeking information from authoritative sources and that my experiences are honestly presented as I remember them.

I was born July 7, 1942, in Thompson-Johnson Hospital in Elberton, delivered by Dr. Walton Johnson, (no kin) to my parents F. A. (Shine) and Lucile (Cleveland) Johnson. At that time my parents lived in the Palmetto community of Oglethorpe County, but by September that year they had moved back into Elberton. We lived in several rental houses before moving to North Oliver Street when I was in the second grade. My parents lived there until after I married and had a child. I had a brother six years older, and a sister three years younger. We were a happy, loving family.

Growing up we played with all the neighbor children along the street. We walked across the nearby deep branch on a one-by-twelve board. Since the branch flowed under the street we sometimes followed it to the other side. Daddy had a garden, and we planted, hoed and picked.

I walked to Central School and walked, or rode with Mrs. Carrie Dodge, who lived next door, to Sunday School and church. I finally got a bike when I was 11. It was a hand-me-down, but it rode as good as the shiny new one my down-the-street neighbor, Roger Cosby, got for Christmas. He and I rode our bikes to school then in the afternoons we rode up the street to the SAL Railroad Station where we rode in and out around the posts at the paved boarding area. At a machine there, we bought Beemans Gum for a penny.

My family didn't have a car until I was in the seventh grade and my bike often took me to *town*, three blocks up the street, to purchase thread, zippers or other things my mother needed in her seamstress work.

I graduated high school in June 1960 so I know a lot about the '50s as that was the time I became a teenager and thought I knew "everything."

As a young teenager, much too young to date which only happened when you were 16, my friends and I began to stage, what we called *parties*. Every month or so we would invite 'couples' to attend a party at our homes. Our mothers would make Kool-Aid and cookies, and everybody would bring their latest 45 records featuring Elvis, Buddy Holly, Little Richard, The Everly Brothers and others. This marked the beginning of our dating years.

Later we cleaned out the attic of the garage at Rita's house and made it our party place. Mr. Wilbur H. gave us an air-conditioner to be used there.

Thinking back, those friends went on to became teachers, coaches, business owners, doctors, and more; *who would ever have thought?* Some have died, but I am grateful for the great times we had and the memories we share.

After high school graduation, I was off to college for a while, then I married Cecil Bond in 1963. We have a boy and two girls and have been involved in many different activities through their growing-up years. We now have four grandchildren and one great-grandson.

Our group included Stanley A., Sherry B., Maria C., Howard C., Roger C., Dickie E., Billy F., Mary Minor H., Peggy H., Telle H., Rita L., Jack N., Marcia O., Walter S., Howell T., Robert T., and me. As many as could, attended every party; family commitment sometimes interfered.

Chapter 2
Elbert County

In the year 1773, the Indians of upper Georgia had become indebted to the traders of Augusta and Savannah in a sum far exceeding $100,000.

King George III, purchased in that year a large tract of land for approximately $200,000 from the Creeks and Cherokees. This tract included the present counties of Elbert, Wilkes, Hart, Oglethorpe, Lincoln and portions of Greene, Taliaferro and Madison. The treaty of purchase was made at Augusta July 1, 1773 and this territory became known as the "Ceded Lands." Enough of the purchase price was withheld to pay the Indian's obligations to the traders. In the year 1777, all the Ceded Lands were, by the State Constitution, created/named Wilkes County.

The first real settlement to be made upon Elbert County soil was that at Dartmouth which stood on the point area where the Broad and Savannah River meet. It developed into a small village of people moving into the area from the Carolinas. It was of sufficient importance to command the erection of a stockade, called Fort James, for its protection. A land court was held at Dartmouth from September

1773 through June 1775, for the purpose of disposing of the Ceded Lands.

In the spring of 1776, fifty well mounted and equipped rangers manned Fort James. The supplies listed for each ranger consisted of a rifle, two pistols, a hanger, a powder horn, a shot pouch and a tomahawk.

Petersburg

In year 1784, Gen George Mathews, who later became a Georgia governor, brought many Virginians and North Carolinians to this Broad and Savannah River country, in what later became Elbert County, and they established themselves in the territory expanding that village of Dartmouth.. It soon became the thriving and commercially important town of Petersburg.

During 1790–1830 it flourished as THE commercial center for Elbert County. The property, outside the village boundaries, initially was leased for the tobacco trade. As tobacco had to be inspected before sold, there were several warehouses to inspect this staple crop before it was floated down river in the flat-bottomed Petersburg Boats to Augusta.

On January 1, 1795, a post office was established there for Petersburg had become a thriving town of over 2,000 permanent residents. Stores, shops and two taverns were erected, and it soon became second in importance to Augusta in the upper Georgia area. "In summer numbers of persons from Savannah, Darien and other points in the lower country visited Petersburg for the gay social life and for the purpose of drinking the water of a famous Lithia spring in the vicinity." Several social clubs were organized in Petersburg and the Masonic Lodge was said to have been the second established in Georgia, after Savannah. Two U.S. Senators, William Wyatt Bibb and Judge Charles Tait were from Petersburg. This is the only instance in the history of the United States when two men served simultaneously from the same town.

After the War of 1812 many of its citizens moved west toward newly opened land. Then cotton became the most important product of the area and it did not need to be inspected. There were a series of floods in the town and many of the home basements had standing water for a period as no way to drain water. Malaria Yellow Fever resulted and many townspeople who were left contracted the disease and died and it was virtually abandoned by start of the Civil War.

While the Clark Hill Dam was being built at Augusta, a genealogical survey was conducted because the town area would be under backwater when the dam became operational. After the survey was complete the graves at the town site were transferred to the cemetery area of Bethlehem Methodist Church which is just off Highway 72 between Elberton and Calhoun Falls.

Bobby Brown State Park marks the site of the old town which is now under the water of Clark Hill Lake. Several times when the backed waters were at a low stage my husband and I traveled to Petersburg, and to Lisbon, which was across the Broad River in Lincoln County, where we saw evidences of the houses and found pieces of pottery, etc.

Ruckersville

Ruckersville is now on the National Register of Historic Places. To reach it, travel out Georgia #368 from Elberton towards Starr, South Carolina.

It was founded by the same Rucker family who founded Ruckersville Virginia. John Rucker and several other aristocrats traveled from Virginia, through the Carolinas to Georgia and settled near Van's Creek in 1793. Ruckersville is several miles up the Savannah R. from Petersburg.

The town grew to 600-700 residents, having 50 stores, two banks, two schools, one Academy, whose principal was a Princeton graduate, and a newspaper.

Joseph Rucker, John's son, and James Rucker, kin but not brothers, owned the two banks. The one owned by Joseph was so widely used that it became a Georgia institution as it handled financial dealings between Augusta and Savannah. By its business, Joseph, who was born in 1788, became Georgia's first millionaire.

It was the destination center for the Savannah R. pole-boats which brought goods upriver from Savannah. (Know what pole-boats were? Were these same as flat bottom ones used at Petersburg?) It was one of the five chief towns of Georgia which were all along the river–Savannah, Augusta, Petersburg, Edinburg and Ruckersville.

Ruckersville was also the birthplace of Joseph Rucker Lamar who, at his death, was an Associate Justice of the U.S. Supreme Court.

A little side story–Ruckersville was home of a Mrs. Wall who feared that at the time of her death no preacher would be available for her service. So, when an itinerant preacher came to town, she had him preach her funeral, with her in attendance.

You know about Savannah and Augusta. I've already talked about Petersburg and Ruckersville but of the small village of Edinburg there is no tract to be found. It was between Petersburg and Ruckersville near Gregg Shoals on the Savannah River. The area was named for John Gregg, who owned large acreage and was one of the first settlers there.

Elberton

By legislative action on December 10, 1790, Elbert County was created from Wilkes County. They chose a small settlement formed in 1769, that William Woodley's family and a few others stopped at a spring located in a ravine, and that the group of weary travelers found the water from the spring so invigorating that they settled in the area, naming the site of Old Town Springs. Woodley and his family then built a house on the hill overlooking the spring. (*In 1969* the *Elberton chapter of the DAR placed a marker on the site of this first known dwelling in Elberton. Which has now been 'misplaced'*). On January 20, 1791, the first session of Elbert County Superior Court was held at the home of Thomas A. Carter, on Beaverdam Creek, some four miles northwest of Elberton. George

Walton, a signer of the Declaration of Independence, was the presiding judge. This house later burned.

It was during this first term that James Meredith was indicted, tried and convicted of the offense of murder. He was hanged on February 22, 1791. So the first legal execution in Elbert County took place less than three months after its formation. At the same court session George Walker, Thomas Carter and Josiah Walton were presented for profane swearing and Elieu Post was presented for selling spirits.

On June 5, 1791 the Commissioners of Elbert County purchased 40 acres of land from John Baker. This acreage included the "town spring" which is now located under the Granite Bowl. Probably built on the high side of a ravine near where current courthouse is located, a combined courthouse and jail, probably built of logs, was constructed during the year 1791.

In 1955, the Georgia Historical Society installed a marker on the grounds of the present courthouse showing that beginning in 1788 the road from Elberton to Lexington GA, which was called the Old Post Road, was the one along which Post Riders traveled to deliver mail from one town to the other. "Stocks for local merchants were brought over this road until 1878 when the first railroad came to Elberton" is stated on the sign.

In the early days houses were few in Elberton. They were mainly built in the area of the present town square with the second courthouse occupying the square center. "The courtroom in this building served as a ballroom for many festive dances and other events." (*Third courthouse which is the present one was built in 1894, see cover picture*). The first building to be constructed of Elbert County's granite was the old jail that stood on the corner of Oliver Street and College Avenue. Elberton was incorporated by the Georgia Legislature in 1803.

There were no hotels/motels and an application was granted to Beverly Allen on February 23, 1803, "Do herewith permit you to keep a tavern to your own dwelling house."

Rates Were As Follows:

Dinner	$0.31½
Supper	$0.25
Breakfast	$0.25
Lodging	$0.12½
Stableage	$0.12½
Corn/oats, per gallon	$0.12½
Fodder, per bundle	$0.03
Jamaican Rum, per gallon	$3.43
Brandy, per gallon	$3.00
Whiskey, per gallon	$2.00
Cider, per gallon	$0.50

In the early 1800s Elbert County was "heavily endowed" with slaves because it was almost completely made up of farms and "plantations."

During the Civil War 1861-1865 portions of the 15th, 37th, and 38th Georgia Infantry Regiments had companies from Elbert County. Many men from the county fought in the war. Gen. Sherman's troops by-passed Elbert County sparing destruction of homes and businesses.

Did you know Elbert County, in the past, had a brickyard? It was located on the still named Brickyard Road which is to right of Highway #17 N between Dewy Rose and Bowman. It was in operation from the 1890s until 1918 and bricks from there were fabricated from kaolin dug from the banks of the upper area of Beaverdam Creek. These bricks were shipped to many areas by railroad. W. O. Jones was involved in its ongoing work. Bricks from there were used in the construction of the present courthouse, the Seaboard Depot and Central School.

During the Presidency of Franklin Roosevelt, through the Works Progress Administration the Armory Auditorium was built. The basement held all their offices and equipment. The main floor was used for their soldiering. Later, 1950s, the upstairs was used as the basketball court of Elberton High School which was next door to the Auditorium.

Elberton has been in the granite business since the early 1900s. There are now at least 57 granite plants who are members of the EGA and there are many companies that broker granite and those who purchase granite, as from China, and sell to local plants.

The county has decreased in population in the past few years. I remember when car tags showed that Elbert County was #50 in Georgia's population. Last census it was #99!

Facts from: "History of Elbert County" John H. McIntosh

"Old Petersburg and Broad River of Georgia"   E. Merton Coulter

"Georgia Landmarks, and Legends" Knight

"Elbert County" Images of America Joyce M. Davis

"The Architectural Legacy of Elberton"   Joyce M. Davis

Read "Beneath These Waters: Archaeological and Historical Studies of 11,500 Years Along the Savannah River?" Between 1969-1985 the National Park Service and U.S. Army Corps of Engineers conducted this survey of 28 miles between Elbert and Hart Counties in Georgia and Anderson and Abbeville Counties in SC. Over the years 730 historical/prehistoric sites were located and uncovered at Gregg Shoals, Rucker's Bottoms, Beaverdam Creek, Harper's Ferry, Van Creek and McCalla Bottoms.

Chapter 3
The Elberton Square

Elberton, similar to most other small towns, was laid out around a town square which in the 1950s ours was divided into four sections with paved walkways lengthwise and crosswise. There were four huge oak trees, one in each section, and the trees were surrounded by wooden benches with high backs. On Saturday afternoons those benches would be filled with husbands sitting around '*solving the world problems*' while their wives did the weekly shopping.

The square later received the name of "Sutton Square" in memory of Mr. Ben Sutton who worked to accomplish the beautification of Elberton's square area and was very instrumental in the work of changing the town's spring and gulley into the nationally recognized Granite Bowl

On July 15, 1898, the first Confederate soldier statue, carved of granite, was installed at the center of the square. It got the nickname "Dutchy" because many people thought it looked like a Pennsylvania Dutchman. The statue was pulled down in August 1900, and buried near the base on which it had been standing.

A second Confederate monument, made of white bronze (zinc), was dedicated on April 19, 1905, and was placed on the base from which "Dutchy" had been toppled. This is the one that stands on the Elberton Square.

"Dutchy" was unearthed in April 1982, and after clean-up, was placed in the Elberton Granite Association museum on College Avenue where it is still located.

Inscribed on that base of the statue is:

East side

Inscription of a Confederate Flag   "1861-1865"

"Elbert County to Her Confederate Dead"

North side

Elbert County to her Confederate Dead
Cornerstone Laid by Grand Lodge of Georgia
July 15, 1898, John H. Jones A.G.M.
"Let the stranger who in future times reads
This Inscription, Recognize that these were
men Whom power could not corrupt, Whom Death
could not terrify, Whom defeat could not dishonor.
Let the Georgia of another generation
Remember that the State taught them how
To live and how to Die and that from their
Broken fortunes she had preserved for her
Children the priceless treasures of their
Memories.

West side

This Monument perpetuates the memory of
Those who true to the instinct of their birth
Faithful to the teachings of their Fathers
Constant in their love of the South,
Died in the performance of their Duty.

South side

These men have Glorified a fallen cause,
By the simple manhood of their lives the
Patient endurance of Suffering and the

Heroism of Death, and who in the Dark
Hours of imprisonment in the Hopelessness
Of the Hospital found support and consolation
In the belief that at home they would not be
Forgotten.
(Capitalization as on monument)

Mrs. R. M. Heard and her collaborators
Have erected this monument.

Also, there is a plaque cemented in the eastern side of the center walk stating:

Site
First County House
Elbert County
1795
DAR

On the western side there is another imbedded plaque which states:

In The Year 1990 A.D. Elbert County
Celebrated its 200th Anniversary. To
Commemorate The Bicentennial Occasion
A Time Capsule Filled With Historical Items
Was Buried Here On December 10. 1990 AD.
This Capsule Is To Be Opened By Citizens Of
Elbert County On December 10, 2040 AD.

The square has had several renovations and today (2019) there is only a walkway across the middle of the square with the statue in the middle. There are iron benches along the walkway with individual dedications.

1. Dedicated to the Love of Gardening   2007 Iris Garden Club Founded 1950
2. Given By Reddie and Miss Ellie Mae   2007
3. In Honor of W. Marvin "Daddy" Hardy A downtown Elberton Fixture For More Than Half a Century

Either end of the Square is a grassy area with four large trees. Also on either end there are two granite benches with the inscription of "Sutton Square." In the midst of these two benches there is a round planter of granite with a decorative light pole in its center

How many times have you driven around the square in Elberton? What about the semi-circle that is at the north end of the square–what's on it? I'm sure you'll say "there is a fountain" but what else? Do you know which tribes of Indians originally lived in this area? Do you know when Elberton was formed? Do you know how many Elbert county residents died in the Civil War, or in World War I? Do you know why the county seat was placed in this location? Do you know when the first train came into Elberton?

There are many more questions I could ask but if you wish to know the answers to the ones I've listed all you need to do is visit the fountain area and read the thirteen inscriptions on the granite walls that surround the fountain. Or, finish reading this article and you will know.

At the north end of Sutton Square there is a half-moon shaped area where the fountain stands. There is a paved walkway leading to the fountain that has a granite bench on either side with inscriptions. Left side bench:

Member Firms of the Elberton Granite Association Contributing To Building of Bicentennial Memorial Fountain – 1976

(Then 46 firm names are engraved.)

At Right side:

Others Contributing to Building of Bicentennial Memorial Fountain – 1976

City of Elberton   Elbert County   Designer Ben Smith
Sculptor Dario Rossi

General Contractor Suttles Construction   EGI Employees
Turner Concrete Company

The fountain has thirteen granite sides with the following inscriptions:

BEFORE 1776 EARLY SETTLERS

Elbert County Was A Portion Of The Hunting And Burial Grounds Of The Cherokee And Creek Indians. Early Settlers Came From North Carolina and Virginia. First Settlement At Dartmouth Prior To 1773, Later known As Petersburg. Located At "The Point" Where Broad And Savannah Rivers Joined.

1776-1783 REVOLUTIONARY WAR PERIOD

Elbert County Area Was Part Of Wilkes County. Colonial Patriots Included Stephen Heard, Later Governor Of Georgia, Benjamin Hart, Dan Tucker, And Others. Nancy Hart, A Famous Revolutionary Heroine, Lived Near Broad River and Performed Magnificent Deeds Of Bravery and Military Feats.

1783-1790 PETERSBURG ERA

Petersburg, Established By Dionysius Oliver, Became A Major Early Georgia Town Of 2,000 Population. Site Covered By Waters Of Clark Hill Lake In 1950s. Two Of Petersburg Residents, Dr. William Wyatt Bibb And Judge Charles Tait, Served Simultaneously In The U. S. Senate In 1813. The Only Instance In History That Two Senators Lived In Same Town.

1790 ELBERT COUNTY ESTABLISHED

On December 10, 1790 Elbert County Was Created From Wilkes County By Act Of The Georgia Legislature. Named For

General Samuel Elbert, Revolutionary Soldier and Governor Of Georgia. First Session Of Elbert County Superior Court Was Held On January 20, 1791, At The Home Of Thomas A. Carter On Beaverdam Creek.

1790-1860 A TIME OF GROWTH

Elbert Count's Population Increased Rapidly. Land was cleared and roads were built. Cotton Replaced Tobacco as the principal farm crop. Churches were organized – Van's Creek, Doves Creek and Falling Creek Baptist; Bethlehem, Coldwater, Stinchcomb, Elberton and Eliam Methodist; along with and others. Heardmont and Ruckersville were settled and Joseph Rucker established the Nationally Famous Bank of Ruckersville.

1803 CITY OF ELBERTON CREATED

Elberton Was Established By The Georgia General Assembly On December 10, 1803. Site Selected As County Seat Because It Was Near The Center Of The Area. Located On A Natural Watershed, Well Elevated, With A Good Drinking Water Spring.

1860-1878 CIVIL WAR AND RECONSTRUCTION

Elbert County Furnished Many Troops To The Confederate Cause – 189th and 202nd Georgia Militia, Fireside Guards, Bowman Volunteers, McIntosh Volunteers, and Others. Over 280 Of Their Men Gave Their Lives In Battle. Elbert Was A Banner County Of Georgia During The Reconstruction Period, Steadfast In Its Opposition To Radicalism.

1878-1900 RAILROADS AND GRANITE BEGINNINGS

First Railroad In Elbert County, From Elberton To Toccoa, Completed In 1878. Another Line To Atlanta And Richmond Was Finished in 1891, Opening Up New Opportunity For Commerce And Trade. The Elberton Granite Industry Was Started With The Opening Of Commercial Quarries In 1889, Followed By Small Finishing Plants. Elberton Gradually Became Known As "The Granite City."

1900-1920 ECONOMIC AND CULTURAL EXPANSION

Public School System Organized: Many Schools Built. Churches Expanded; Cultural Groups Organized; Farming Flourished; Elberton Became Trade Center. Bowman And Middleton Incorporated. World War I Supported By Elbert Countians; 24 Gave Their Lives In The Service Of Their Country. Joseph Rucker Lamar, Ruckersville Native, Appointed To U. S. Supreme Court In 1911.

1920-1940 BOOM AND DEPRESSION

Prices of Cotton And Land Reached New Highs, Followed By New Lows. Banks Closed And Reopened. Elberton's Industrial and Granite Base Helped To Ease The Depression Woes. Chamber of Commerce Organized; Civic Clubs Formed; Highways Built; Automobiles, Electricity, Telephones and Other Conveniences Became Commonplace.

1940-1960 NEW PROSPERITY

Elberton's Booming Granite Industry Set Economic Pace For Area. Elberton Granite Association Formed. Homes And Businesses Increased In Number Through Out The City and County. Medical Facilities Enlarged. World War II and Subsequent Conflicts Claimed Lives Of 53 From Elbert County. Development of Savannah River Hydroelectric Projects Begun Under Leadership Of Congressman Paul Brown.

1960-1970 COMMUNITY OF PROGRESS

Granite Centers Municipal Complex, Granite Bowl, Civic Center, New School Buildings, Churches, Banks, Recreational Facilities And Shopping Centers Built. Industry More Diversified With Expansion Of Employment Opportunities. Active Community - Boosting Organizations Encouraged Progress For "Ever Expanding" Elberton And Elbert County.

1776-1996 TWO CENTURIES OF ADVANCEMENTS

From America's Founding In 1776 to its Bicentennial Year Of 1976, The Story of Elbert County Is One Of Steady Advancement And Progress – In Agriculture and Industry, In Development of Natural Resources, In Educational and Cultural Activities, In Religious and

Political Endeavors, And In Improving The Quality Of Life Enjoyed By All Its Citizens.

Inside the thirteen sides bubbles a fountain. In the middle of the water is a stacked group of three granite blocks, each of smaller dimensions as they rise. As you approach the fountain you note their inscriptions.

As you walk forward the inscription reads:

Elberton Granite Bicentennial Memorial Fountain Commemorating the 200th Anniversary of American Independence 1976-1976.

This inscription is repeated on the opposite side.

Right side reads:

Erected During 1976 As A Gift To Elberton and Elbert County by Members of Elberton Granite Association, Inc. "May this fountain serve as an everyday reminder of the Elbert Granite Industry's interest in this community and contributions to this areas economies and Civic Life."

Left side reads:

Dedicated To All Citizens Of Elberton And Elbert County * Past * Present * Future *

Who Love The United States Of America and

Cherish Its Ideals Of Life, Liberty and The Pursuit Of Happiness.

On the pinnacle block a decorative design surrounds all sides and a beautifully carved granite eagle sits atop the summit

Everyone should stop and look at the fine work that encompasses all.

Chapter 4
Around the Square
Elberton's 1950s Era
West Side

The Strand Theater, located where Franklin Finance now stands, burned with such a ferocious fire that the Washington, Georgia fire department came to help extinguish it. After it burned, and the lot was cleared, Mr. Willie Moon sat atop a large pole similar to a telephone pole, installed by Milton Butler and others of city Light and Water Department, as a local promotion for the movie "Sitting Pretty." Mr. Moon sat atop the pole for 30 days with a telephone at the top, and one at ground level where you could call asking him questions. If you went by the location and did not find him upon the pole, you would win a prize. What was the prize? Was it ever won? By whom? I've not found the answer to these questions.

First Franklin Finance, 2 Oliver Street, has incorporated the building to the right of them into their office space. That portion formally housed the "Hot Spot" and before that, Western Auto, owned by Hugh Maffett, telephone #1188.

Teasley (Clyde) and Brown (Julian) Insurance, telephone #532, was where The Big Pink Bow is located. Jane G. Webb and Barbara Outz worked in that insurance office.

Next door was The Diana Shop where Tena's main entrance is. Mrs. Anna Nicora was the first manager followed by Mrs. Ben McLanahan, Jr. Mrs. Don (Pat) Kellum worked there after her high school classes. This location formally housed "The Maxwell House," which later became "The Piedmont Hotel."

End store, by courthouse drive, has had many occupants, J. C. Poole's Men's Store, Jay's Footware, Drake's Watch Repair, Shorty's and The English Cottage. The store is empty. It was also part of The Maxwell House Hotel.

South Side

The Samuel Elbert Hotel is on the southwest corner of Elberton's square. It originally opened in September 1925. After closing as a hotel, Walter McNeeley once ran a men's clothing shop in the former lobby and Norman Suddeth ran a restaurant on the ground floor. For many years Southeastern Power Administration, Underwriters Insurance and The Elbert Examiner occupied space in the building. After much renovation it re-opened as a hotel in March 2017.

Next to the hotel is a small building, 6 Public Square, where Elberton Savings and Loan began, and where Peyton Hawes Law Office were once located. It has recently been occupied by Elcon but is owned by the City of Elberton.

Mr. Joe Allen built the next building for his Dry Goods business. J. C. Poole later purchased this building and it opened at Christmas, 1948, by Mr. Poole's son-in-law Marvin Hardy as the first Poole Store in Elberton. There is an advertisement painted on the outside of the building as seen from behind the hotel.

Ward's Pharmacy fills this spot with a third generation, Bob Ward, serving as the pharmacist.

Paul Radin operated the Jewel Box. Now the Georgia Coaches Athletic Association fills that spot.

The marble front building next was originally the "Bank of Elberton." McLanahan Quarries offices later occupied it. Now Harper Quarries offices occupies it.

Next are stairs up to "Miss Maggie's" Millinery Shop. Her shop was moved to several locations.

Grocery stores occupied the next two buildings. T.T. Thornton and Son, telephone #33, where groceries were delivered by Otha on a bicycle with a big basket, and Hewell's Grocery at 16 South Public Square, telephone #487 which was owned by L. D. Hewell. Bill Yarbrough remembers that his mother regularly ordered groceries from Hewell's, and sometimes she would order him an ice cream. He would stand out in his front yard (Highland Park) and watch for the bicycle coming to deliver the groceries. He could see it coming about two blocks away and couldn't wait for his ice cream. It was in a round cardboard cup with a wooden spoon and the grocer would have specially wrapped it–but most of the time it would still be melted. Bill enjoyed it anyway. Both grocers were where Begley's Mercantile stands.

After the grocery stores, Gallant Belk Company next filled those areas. In the 50s heavy plastic air tubes were at each station where a purchase was made. The bill of sale and money for the purchase were placed in a metal container and sent through the air pipe tubes to the main office where the payment was noted and needed change was returned to the location of purchase in the same manner. This was like current bank drive-ins.

There was a "Shoe-Store Fluoroscope" that used x-ray to show how your foot would fit within a shoe so you would know which size to purchase. Stan's Music and S & S Collectibles occupy these spots.

On the right side of this building you could barely see a huge painted sign for Coca-Cola. During 2018 this sign was restored with paint. This sign was repainted in 2019.

The corner store, before it became a part of Gallant-Belk, was Goodman-Peskin, men's clothing store. When Jamie Parsons served as a nurse at Central Elementary/High School and she found a child that needed clothing to attend school, or medical correction (such as a tonsillectomy) Mr. Peskin had set up an account for her to use to address these needs. When the account balance was low, she went to him, and he added to the account. (This was NOT to be told by Ms.

Parsons and was learned only after Mr. Peskin's death.) This section was later purchased by Gallant-Belk and made into their men's clothing area. Papa's Pizza is located there.

East Side of Square

McLanahan Chevrolet was in a small building, with a chain-link fence across the front of the property with the address of 19 South McIntosh Street. This building was demolished and the area became a parking lot for the Dixie-Home Store which was in the first building. Public dances were held in the parking lot on Saturday night. Later a building was built on the parking lot property that housed the office and service area of Ed Shive Tire.

Next was Dixie-Home Grocery. That store has been divided and Cleveland Shoes operated in left side. Today Adrian's A Cut Above The Rest is there and the right side store is an ice cream shop.

There was a Woolworth's Five and Ten, 9 East Public Square, telephone #782-W, where "Fashion USA" is now located. Woolworth's had moved from beside First National Bank on the north side of the square. Gilbert McDonald was manager, Martha Johnson served as secretary/treasurer and clerks were Helen Irwin Annie Ruth Rucker and Mrs. McDaniel. Ann (Williams) Gunter worked there at Christmas.

C & M Thrift now occupies the next store.

Charles Riley's Men's Shop, later Hill (Leonard) and Harper (Harry C.) Men's Shop was where Georgia Center for Sight is now located.

The next store now occupied by Blume Hair and Co. formerly housed (Ralph) Cousins Jewelry, telephone 660. The 1956 telephone directory listed its address only as East Public Square. It was later addressed as 3 South McIntosh Street

On the corner of square and Heard Street a Shell service station was built in 1933. Over the years it served as the first Greyhound/Trailways Bus Stop in Elberton. At a later date Star

Cleaners had a drop off/pick up spot there. Before moving, the Elberton Chamber of Commerce used its location for their offices.

Patz and Fortson, clothing store, was on the eastern corner of Heard and McIntosh St's. William and Dorothy Fortson ran it. The section of the store on North McIntosh sold appliances and Albert (Mutt) Gaines was manager. At different times the upstairs held Mrs. Echols beauty shop and Miss Maggie's Millinery. Attached to this building, but facing Heard Street, Mr. Henry Thompson ran a small grocery store in the building where Phil Johnson Insurance is now located.

North Side of Square

Granite City Bank, telephone #7, stood on the corner of the square and South McIntosh, where the "Star" Office stands. Bank officers and workers were: Mr. Furman Smith, President; Frank Fortson, Vice President; James Cleveland, Juette Bond, Hugh Jackson, Mary Frances Fortson, Mrs. Roberts and Jeanne C. Phelps.

Elberton Drug, telephone #424, owned by James Robert Lee, filled the spot to the left of the bank. The left side of the drugstore was filled with anything/everything–a small, earlier Walmart–and the right side was a soda shop and eating area with stools at a counter. Attached to the dividing wall of each individual booth was a metal/plastic box that inside had "pages" you turned to find the songs you wanted played on the juke box. You deposited your quarter in the slot, punched the correct button for your song and soon it would play!

I received a call from a lady, Patricia (Beggs) McBrayer of Carrollton, Georgia who had received a package from Elberton and the item inside had been wrapped in a copy of "The Elberton Star." She is from Elberton and she began reading it to see what was going on in our city. The paper included an article about Elberton Drug and in her call she said she had worked there before graduating high school in 1944. She said that Dr. Ingram and Dr. Gene Shirley were the pharmacists and the waitresses were Mabel Shumate, who always wore her hair pulled up with curls on top; Mrs. Milton Gillespie, Mrs.

Laura Helton, Ophelia Maxwell and Juanita Parham. Mr. Milton Gillespie ran the grill and Norris David and James Moon ran the fountain. Mrs. Ellison was the cashier. She stated that Sara Haslett, Martha Ann Dewberry and Margaret Dewberry worked as clerks. Mrs. Ellison and Mrs. Clark were cashiers. Over several years the Gillespie boys, Marshall, Tommy, Jack, Billy and Milton Jr. worked at various jobs in the store.

Mrs. Ellison, first name Leslie, was a tiny lady who wore her hair pulled into a bun at the base of her neck and waves were set in her hair all over her head. She used curved metal clamps with teeth in them to set waves in her hair. Do you remember those clamps? What were they called? Her husband was W. W. Ellison head of the city Electric Department. At times she was the caretaker of her niece Mary Coile (Brown) Barden.

Sanford Cole remembered working at Elberton Drug in the mid-fifty's, making $19 a week, delivering prescriptions on a bike. One he particularly remembers is delivering a 10 cent pack of bobby pins to a home in the Elberton Mill Village and it was almost dark when he returned to the store. He bought his first car, which cost him $250, while working there. His hours were 5 am-5 pm, or 11 am to 11 pm, which totaled 66 hours a week. Back then it was the only place in town to order breakfast; he remembers Claude Ray and Everett Saggus coming there every morning for coffee and breakfast.

Colonial Jewelers at 17½ Public Square, owned by Curtis Morrow, was in the narrow shop which was next and their telephone number was 281-R. At one time Sam Phelps shoe store was located there. The store is now empty.

Roses Department Store (as listed in the City Directory Volume 3) 13 North Public Square, filled the spot where Sanders CPA is now located. Roses had a 1 cent candy counter with loose candy under glass and you could pick out how many of each you wanted. They also had a machine that popped popcorn, fresh every couple of hours. The wooden floors were soaked with an oil mixture rather than being painted. Milton Butler, as a 15-year-old part-time worker there, had the "opportunity" of spreading oil on those floors as part of his job. Edna Goodwin worked there after school and her husband to be, Marco, came by bringing her an engagement ring. She wouldn't accept it at first because she thought he was joking, and that it was one of the fake rings for sale at Roses. She later realized it was real, and they were married for 50 plus years.

There is a painted advertisement on the James Street side of this building. "Spearmint" is partly visible. Can you make out more?

Next James Street enters the square area and several businesses were on it.

The doorway to the first set of stairs on the left behind Herndon's was the entrance to Elberton Labor Council, Granite Cutters International Association, AFL-CIO, whose office and meeting area was above Herndon's drug. That logo is still printed on the first of the second-story windows on James Street. F. A. Johnson, then Albert Norman, were union reps for GCIA. It was also the meeting place of LOCAL 574, AFL-CIO International Ladies' Garment Workers' Union, and LOCAL 85 AFL United Textile Workers of America. This space is now occupied by Steve Mooney, sculptor extraordinaire lives there. He sometimes places paintings on windows of eating establishments and other businesses.

The second door behind Herndon Drug led to the office of Ben Sutton Real Estate, 14 James Street, phone #223-W, for whom Sutton Square is named and who was instrumental in construction of the Granite Bowl football stadium. Currently Prosurfaces Corporation is there.

T. P. Wooten State Farm Insurance was at 14 James Street, #223-W. (The 1956 telephone directory states the same address for these last two.)

There was a small building on the right. I'm told that was called the Rogers Building. At one time mules for farming were sold there. Also at one time Mr. Zach Rogers had a Hospital Equipment Company on James Street. This building has been demolished. Did both occupy the same building?

Herndon's Drug Store was on the corner of square and James Street and their telephone was #84 or #85. James Moon worked behind the counter and you could purchase a Lemon Sour there. On James Street side you can still read "HERNDONS Soda and Cigars Drugs and Candy." I can't make out all the painted advertisement. This store space is now occupied by Net Core Labs Computer Sales and Service.

Next door the Maxwell family operated Elberton Department Store which sold clothes for the complete family. The family also operated a funeral business and caskets were stored upstairs. This later became Poole's Ladies Store run by H. M. Williams who was another son-in-law of Mr. J. C Poole. It is now occupied by Elite Vapor.

The next store was where Woolworth was first located and there was a back entrance coming from the Oliver Street doorway. Inside that doorway you had to decide if you wished to enter Woolworth's, the back side of First National Bank, the small Western Union office that was at this level, take stairs to the basement barber shop or take the elevator or stairs to the upper floors.

Sears Roebuck at one time occupied this same space telephone #1520. It had many washers, dryers, refrigerators, etc. in stock–no clothing, but you could order clothing and other items, from the catalog.

Metal pipes which curved back toward the building, stuck up 6 inches through the sidewalk at the front of Sears store. These were ventilator pipes for the basement and men would gather there, lean on the building, prop their foot on pipes and discuss the world's problems.

The First National Bank stood on the corner of the square and Oliver Street. The bank President was Mr. Hunter. Workers there were

P. C. Maxwell, Mrs. Bill Walton and Mrs. Maude Mashburn. Areas of bank and Sears are currently occupied by "Trendy Retail"

The third floor of this corner building housed the "Elberton Hospital" operated under the auspices of Miss Jean McGinty. Doctors were Dr. D. V. Bailey, Dr. Fletcher Smith, Dr. A. S. Johnson, Dr. Joe Johnson, Dr. D. North Thompson and Dr. Walton Johnson. Ambulances came into "Ambulance Alley" which ran between the same building and the Star Office building, to deliver patients.

On second floor dentists Dr. Charles Johnson and Dr. John Jenkins had their offices. My family patronized Dr. "Charlie" and he DID NOT use Novocain! After drilling he would laugh at your distress and say "It didn't hurt me a damn bit." Dr. Charlie Johnson, dentist, and Dr. Walton, Johnson, M.D. were brothers.

Oliver Street from Square

Basement of the First National Bank building. Currently Anderson's Barber Shop and The Alteration Shop occupy the store areas. It was always the delight of every child to walk down into, then up the steps at opposite end of this "basement" corridor, rather than walk on the regular sidewalk.

Ambulance Alley former office of "The Elberton Star," at 10 Oliver Street, telephone number was 71, is now empty.

10½ is a stairway to upstairs, over 10 Oliver Street. It is now empty.

Weatherly Furniture Co., telephone #503, was located in next two buildings, 15 and 16 Oliver Street. Currently, Shoe In Dance is located at #15 and Re-Max is in #16. Weatherly Furniture had a large elevator, with a rope pulley, to move furniture for storage from main floor to second floor. There are approximately 30 steps to reach the second floor. Although unusable, this elevator is still in place in building #16.

When the #15 store was in operation, the brick wall on the left was covered with some type of plastering. It has since been removed and inside the Re-Max office you can read an advertisement painted on this wall. "MILLIONS Chew Schnapps Tobacco." This same ad is painted on the front of the former building on New Street. At the second floor level of that wall "Hudgins & McIntosh" is painted. Evidently the current left inside wall of Re-Max was the outside wall of the building previously next door.

Worley's Dry Cleaning was located at 18 Oliver Street, where the EGA monument display now stands. George Worley's son said that the company also had an elevator similar to the one at Weatherly's. Mr. J. T Brooks drove a company truck around town to pick-up and deliver laundry. His nose had been cut in a sawmill accident and a portion of one of his thumbs was removed to use as a replacement for the side of his nose. The company was run by Mr. Herman and wife Etta George Worley with help from their sons John and George (Buddy). The family lived in the second house out Railroad Street from Highland Avenue.

There was an Amoco filling station to the left of Worley's Cleaners. It occupied the corner of then Elbert and Oliver Streets. It was run by Mr. Ben McLanahan and his son Ben Jr. and D. C. Richardson worked there. Ben Jr., later ran the Jule Parham Texaco station on lower Heard Street. Mr. Richardson later ran a station/grocery on the corner of Railroad Street and North Oliver, beside Southern Railroad's turn-around.

From College Avenue to public square

On the corner of College Avenue and Oliver Street was Cosby's Lunch Room. The address was 15 North Oliver Street, and telephone was #947. "Famous" hot dogs were sold there. I'm told the kitchen was in the basement and food was sent upstairs on a dumb waiter. Mr. "Peg Leg" Durham, called this because he had a wooden prosthetic leg, racked balls for pool. Presently V and M Sports Club occupies this building.

The next two businesses had the same address, 15 Oliver Street. You stepped onto a paved entrance area then took the door to the right, or to the left, depending upon the business you wished to enter.

Mewbourne (Loyd) and Lee (R.E.) Insurance Agency, telephone #15, was on the right. Edna Williams and Dodo Thornton were their secretaries. Mr. Clyde Williams' Barber Shop was on the left. Martin Bagwell and Cecil Bond worked there as shoe-shine boys when the cost of a shine was 25 cents. Now Kawannas Hair Studio is on the left and V & M Barber Shop #15B is on the right in this building.

Next was Torrey Hardware. Earlier Bond Hardware (Clifford Bond's father) was located in the same building. In 1956, Ace Hardware filled the same location, and was operated by Ralph Taylor. This building's address was 9 Oliver Street. Today Times Square is located there.

Ward's Pharmacy, at 7 Oliver Street, telephone #23, was next to Ace Hardware. It was run by pharmacist Charles Patrick Ward, then by his pharmacist son Robert Ward, Sr., then by his pharmacist grandson Robert, Jr. Near the booths in the area used by adults to enjoy their cola's and ice cream was a round table for children. It was made of wood with a metal band around the edge and had metal legs that flared at the bottom where they sat on the floor. The chairs had wooden seats, banded in metal, heart shaped backs made with the same round metal and legs like the table. Robert Jr., who currently runs Ward's Pharmacy on the south side of the square, said that he still has the table and chairs. The building is now empty

Between the former hardware store and Firestone is a doorway to the stairs which leads upstairs to where the Elks Club first met. It is now being remodeled into apartments.

The next business was Firestone Home and Auto Supplies, run by Mr. George Leard, and owned by Mr. Peyton Hawes. Their address was 1 Oliver Street and telephone was #617. They had radios, TV's, appliances, small furniture and toys, especially at Christmas. For a time, Mr. Hawes' law office was located upstairs. Remember his secretary Mrs. Katherine Yeary? The office for the First Methodist

Church was also upstairs when Sara Kantala was secretary. This building is currently being remodeled into office spaces.

Do You Remember When

Before electric refrigerators the "iceman" delivered ice to individual homes for their ice boxes. The driver would use an ice pick to cut out the correct size, throw a piece of tarpaulin over his shoulder, use tongs to pick up that piece of ice, place it on the tarp and then carry it into the house. He always gave the kids any chips that came loose.

Chapter 5

North McIntosh (One Way) Street

Right side from Square

#4 Patz and Fortson, telephone 363, was on corner. They had a large area of men/women's clothing with narrow gift shop located on Heard Street end. Section located down McIntosh was for household goods, stoves, refrigerators, washers/dryers, etc. Albert Gaines was manager.

#8 Now empty.

#12 M. B. Grimes had Grimes Market grocery store. Now empty.

#14 Next, Mr. A. L Bracey had a hardware store, phone 512, before he was elected tax commissioner. Now empty.

#16 Twin Beauty Shoppe phone 240. Now empty.

#18 Irwin's Department Store, owner Irvin Hite. Now Rooster's.

#20 Now Kathy's Kreations

#22 Now Kathy's Kreations

#24 Now McIntosh Coffee Shop

Belk's Bargain Store occupied the last store before Elbert Street but I have not found their street number. I understand that Tolbert Hood had a furniture business in this location at an earlier date.

North McIntosh, right side from Elbert Street

Elberton Furniture

102 Johnson Hardware/Payne's Hardware, telephone #681, where Ralph Taylor and Charles Ruff worked.

#114 Gholston Hotel, phone 9114. It was built close to train depot for stay of traveling salesmen. Gladys Shepherd is listed as proprietor.

#118 Lucius Carpenter's Dry Cleaners/Laundry, phone 172. Later Paul McCurley – Moving and Transportation Company in this spot, phone 621. At an earlier date Mr. McCurley had a furniture store located on the Square where Hewell's Grocery was later located.

Hoke Almond Radiator Shop and Robinson Motors/Hudson Dealership – later auto repair shop run by Frank Massey and Ora Scarborough

#130 North McIntosh the City Hall, which was built in 1897, stood. An addition was added later.

All of these buildings from 102-130 have been demolished.

New Street is located to left of former City Hall

Mr. Bob McLanahan, retired policeman/Superintendent of City Streets, had coal company on North McIntosh Street, next to railroad tracks. Its location enabled easy unloading from train delivery. He later moved business to Deadwyler Street, phone 853, across from Seaboard Coast Line depot. Wife was Hassie McMullan McLanahan.

Also near the train tracks there was an ice house. Did they have facilities to freeze the ice or was it brought in on a train? Carol G. Walters and Sandra I. Campos used to go there and the owners would let them go inside the freezer section and pick up ice pieces that had fallen off when the blocks were separated. Carol stated how good that was on a hot day!

North McIntosh Street left side from Square

Alley

#9 Reed's Drugstore, then Hiram Scarborough's Pharmacy was in first building beyond alley that is/was behind Granite City Bank building. On Saturday afternoons when we walked to town, mother would take my sister, Eloise, and I there and buy us a chicken salad sandwich which we halved and a Coke. I've never been able to make chicken salad that tastes as good as that tasted! I've been told that for the drugstore Mr. Scarborough's wife made it and egg salad.

Scarborough's Drugstore, telephone #129, later moved to small store in building that formerly housed FBC youth center on Heard Street which was torn down in 2013. Now Salon and Spa.

Next were steps to upstairs location of W.W. Taylor Photography Studio which was later occupied by Photographer Everett Saggus. Being renovated into two upstairs apartments

#11 Railroad Express Agency, telephone #25, Now Square Nails.

Steps. Now being renovated into two upstairs apartments.

#13 Now Sellers Dress Shop

#15 Coggins Shoe Shop, telephone 9121. Now Shelley Welch Cox LLC

#17 J. P Davis Dry Goods phone 540. Now empty

#19 Nash Pool Room phone 9119. Now Richard's Restaurant

#21 James Webb Dry Goods phone 281-W. Now empty

#23 Martin's Café now Consolidated Credit

#25 Charlie Robinson's Shoe Store These two demolished.

#27 Consolidated Credit Corp. Phone 889

North McIntosh left side from Elbert Street

#101 was Powell's Café located at corner of South McIntosh and Elbert Street – The café's front door was for whites only. Entrance for blacks was in back. Food was transported to upstairs kitchen area by a dumbwaiter; pool hall was in back area. Mr. Myerholtz racked balls for pool.

111 was J. S. Warren's Feed Store – where Petal Pusher's is now located

In open area there was a railroad car serving as a café. At one time Jack Ridgeway had a fruit stand in this area also?

#113 North McIntosh was   Loyd's Cafe

What was in the building 3 Reinas Taqueria is presently located? Had it been Myers Market?

Open space

Large building with six entrances -

Mrs. Sew and Sew is at first door.

#123 This was a grocery store (Coward's?) Lunsford Appliance Service was located there.

Eaves Packing – where Walter Eaves began his business. Since individual refrigerators only had a small freezer space this business had freezer storage especially for large amounts of meats.

#127 Joe Roberts Upholstery   His wife Emma and family lived in apartment over Coward's Grocery, per son Andrew Roberts.

All these buildings are to be demolished

In the last building was Thomas J. Sanders Grocery. His wife Alma ran the store for many years after his death. Presently Superior Hair Designs operates there.

Corner of North McIntosh and Deadwyler Street, Frank Whitaker ran filling station, where he began servicing 18 wheelers. Frank's father-in-law, Mr. Ora Clark, had bought the station in approximately 1935, and he sold it to Frank in 1946 after Frank returned from WW II. When Frank built new station on North Oliver, this North McIntosh station was run by D. C. Richardson. Presently a car wash operates there. Info from Mr. Clark's daughter Bobbie Terry.

It seems that there was a big turnover of businesses along this "One Way" street. I've been told the following businesses were there at one time but I've not found their exact addresses.

Birdseye Feed Store, Joyce Oglesby's father ran.

J. P. Allen Shoe store. Was this on Square at one time? Father of Dr. Beverly A. Bond

Roger's Grocery

A & P Grocery where Joe Seymour worked.

A bakery?

Deadwyler Street, left from North McIntosh

Frank Whitaker's station corner with North McIntosh. Now car wash

Mr. Bob McLanahan moved his coal business to location across the street from Seaboard train depot. Mr. McLanahan was murdered at this location.

I.V Carrouth's bicycle shop

Deadwyler Street, right from North McIntosh

Seaboard Airline Railway Station, built 1910, is presently owned by city of Elberton.

"Red" Wilson was attendant and before each train came he hung a bag of railroad instructions on a pole which had a U shaped device at the top with heavy cord between the top of the U's, on which the bag was hung. When train came through engineer, or fireman, would extend their arm through the engine window and catch the cord, which held the bag, in their elbow.

Chapter 6
Elbert Street right side from North Oliver

Corner was gas station run by McLanahan's

James Street was behind it. In Photographer E. W. Saggus photo hanging in "Star" office several buildings shown in this area.

Lee's Pawn Shop. Lee's Pawn was one. What were others?

Elbert Street left side from North Oliver

Sanders Furniture Company, telephone #607. Upstairs had served as a rooming house in the past. There were several wall paintings, painted by a former resident. Discussion was made at time of building's removal, for their recovery. Mr. John Sword used a chain saw to remove the largest picture/wall. It is presently in storage by the city.

Suburban Gas Co. Mr. Arnold Oglesby owner and Mrs. Jimmie (Dixon) Bell was secretary.

Dale Williams Clover Farm Grocery Store was at 17 Elbert Street

Next was alley to backside of Ray Auto.

Powell's Pool Room was on corner with North McIntosh Street

Elbert Street left side from North McIntosh

First building is presently Peanuts Coin Laundry. (New building).

Second business built by George M. Johnson Hardware is now Inglesia de Dios Reino Church

Dew Drop In has been demolished.

Porter & Sons has been demolished.

Bojangles is now closed.

Title Max occupies the building that was built for Hardee's.

Originally there was a small wooden building near the corner with Thomas Street Marvin Broadwell began business there before erecting a permanent building on South McIntosh Street   And Whitlow Electric also began there in '60s.

North Oliver from Elbert Street, right side

Sanders Furniture Co. was on corner but building was removed when Elbert Street was widened.

A Nehi Bottling Plant was located next to Sanders. Owner was I. V. Hulme and Gober Burton was plant operator.

A Bowling Alley was located next to Nehi which also had Pin Ball machines

A 12' wide building was next and Ed Cleveland ran a café there in the 1930s. At later dates car parts were stored there for Ray Auto.

Ray Auto Co.(Chrysler/Dodge/Plymouth), owned by Mr. Fred Ray was next at 122-124 North Oliver telephone phone #174. Beside this store was an alley that led to their service department at the rear.

All these buildings have been demolished and Hop In gas is now in their locations.

The building at 132 North Oliver, with "McLanahan" engraved in stone at roofline, where Thornton's Pawn Shop is now located, was built by brothers Robert, Mack, Dillard and Tenney McLanahan. It was a store for hardware and farm supplies. Later, O. P Cochrane Plumbing, Jule Fortson Plumbing and Charles Ruff Hardware occupied this building.

Next door was The Shanty, which had moved from parking area of gas station near Square. It was operated by Mr. Jack and Mildred Bradford. Its building has now been incorporated into Thornton's Pawn Shop.

Next was two story house with granite wall at sidewalk and granite steps. This was a boarding house at one time. Its steps can still be seen leading to Thornton's present parking area.

Gulf Filling Station, operated by David White. Coy Attaway was attendant.

North Oliver from College Ave., left side

Tom McMullan's Barber Shop. This is where Doug Anderson began his training.

Next was Elberton Firehouse, located where Walgreen's front parking is currently located.

Parker Foster was chief and firemen were: Mack E. Beasley, Alton Carithers, Homer Carithers, Mr. Stratton and later Wayne (Pee Wee) Guest, Donnie Kesler, Joe Johnson and Norman Kelley.

Next was slant faced building, attached to firehouse, where auto parts were stored.

Next was filling station looking building but auto parts were also stored there.

Next, originally Elbert Sales (Ford dealership) operated by John Harris Bailey's father. It was later purchased by Claude Ray and given the name of Claude Ray Ford. It was located in a building to left of present home For Sale at 135 North Oliver Street, where drive to Pinnacle Bank/WalGreens now is located.

All above, from College Avenue, have been demolished.

The brick home located at 135 North Oliver Street is still standing.

In the next lot was a white house which sat near the street but has now been demolished. Its granite wall bordering the sidewalk is still standing with a huge pecan tree in what was the front yard. Barbara Hammond's family lived there when she was a small child. She remembers riding her tricycle up the street to Copeland's Grocery and they would always give her a sucker.

The two story Maxwell's Boarding House set back off North Oliver, in area where M & S Electric now stands at 149 North Oliver Street the family of Harry, Jerry and Jack Shell lived there.

Next, directly on sidewalk was Big Taylor's Fruit Stand. Later, a large building was erected behind the Fruit Stand where Big Taylor's Carpets was located. These both have been demolished but were in area where Ann Jensen Etchings sign and building are located. Now M & S Electric occupies the back portion of this lot.

The large brick building beside the railroad tracks was Copeland's Grocery Warehouse. Owner Mr. Z. W Copeland, had salesmen who traveled a several county area to small stores who placed their orders which the salesmen then delivered to the Warehouse. The next day deliverymen took the filled orders to those small stores. This building has been demolished with only a portion of its brick underpinning showing. Their ad read: "The biggest and most varied line of goods to be found. Come to see us when in the city."

On College Avenue from North Oliver Street, right side

There was a Pure service station on the corner of North Oliver and College Avenue. It was owned by Pure dealer Clyde Brown and run by D. C. Richardson.

Next door was Anderson Auto Parts where Martha Coggin worked as receptionist.

Next door was Pink Garrett's Machine Shop who made tools for the granite industry. These two were only 12' wide shops.

Next was Louree Deadwyler's Flower Shop at 8 College Ave., telephone #581 and her husband Vail, had Elberton Machine Works next door at 12 College Avenue tele. #169

Next was Standard Filling Station 16 College Ave., telephone # 9129 run by brothers V. G., Herman and Jesse Herring. Later was run by brothers James H. and Harley Thomason, then by another set of brothers, Pete and Lanier Anderson.

On the right side of the station was an alley that led to an apartment house where Katherine Harper and her children Larry and Charlotte lived. The house was located about where Pinnacle Bank's ATM now stands. Also there was a large two story house on the hill beside the service station, which is now occupied by Pinnacle Bank.

All this area was purchased in 1951 for erection of First National Bank.

The Fred Herndon's house, which is still standing, was next.

There was a circular drive in front of: the Herndon house, then another two story white house where Jack and Mildred Bradford lived and the drive came back into College Avenue at the W. O. Jones home (Magnolia Estates today).

What is now Magnolia Estates was built in 1905 by W. O. Jones.

The two story home of the R. W. Dyes was next at 92 College Ave.

On the corner of College Avenue and Harper Street sisters Sara Ann and Mary Lizzie Wright lived.

Left on College Avenue from Oliver Street

There is still an alley leading to Courthouse parking behind V. and M Sports Club.

Walton Gaines Pontiac dealership was located at 15 College Avenue, tele. #74. It was owned by Henry Walton and J. E. Gaines. Frank Massey and Pete Anderson worked in the car repair shop. Presently a car repair/painting business is located there. This building started out as a mule barn. Pete Anderson tells that when he worked there for Walton & Gaines that parts were stored in the attic. When one such part was needed, and you climbed the ladder to reach their storage, you also found bales of hay that had been left behind. This building now empty.

Next door there was a Gulf filling station where high school boys gathered each morning before school. It was run by Mr. Starke Hudson.

Beside the station is another alley which runs towards Courthouse parking lot.

Next door was the Mercury dealership owned by John Tom and Joe Edwards and their repair shop was located in the basement where Frank Massey and Cecil Bond worked. Walton Gaines moved to this location when the Mercury dealership went out of business. Later Townhouse Building Supply began in this location and Randall Brady

Plumbing was located downstairs. Today a city park with gazebo is in that location.

Where the parking lot for ECCHS high school gym is presently James Adams' had Elberton Motor Supply.

Next, #41 College Avenue was the brown shingled house Mr. Charlie Johnson, Fire Chief and his daughter Esther, who taught English/Journalism at the high school, lived.

49 College Avenue was Thompson-Johnson Hospital which had 11 patient rooms, 7 single bed and 4 double bed on hospital floor. At first, in the back there was a one room ward that had 3 beds and 1 single room. These last two were turned into a dining room and kitchen when these two were moved. On the hospital floor there was also an X-Ray room, operating room, delivery room and supply room. Downstairs were offices for Dr. D. North Thompson and Dr. Walton Johnson and also a lab. Upstairs from hospital floor, there were two bedrooms for nurses that had two beds in each room. Dot (Bridges) Cecchini and Mrs. Homer Bowdoin were two who lived there for short periods. Out back of the hospital was a building with two apartments where nurses lived. One had a living room, two bedrooms and a bath and Frances Johnson, Mrs. Madden and Betty Jo Poulnott lived there. The second had only two rooms and a bath and Eloise Adams lived there. The hospital had been constructed by additions to the house where Dr. D. North Thompson and his first wife lived.

Next was two story home of Dr. D. North and Mrs. "Miss Emmie" Thompson

Next was Central High and Elementary School which burned in November 7, 1955. At this same location a new high school was built for the first graduating class in 1959. It was later turned into a Middle School when another high school was built on Jones Street After a new middle school was built this facility now houses city/county/state government offices.

Do You Remember When

Few homes had air conditioning so you used a window fan to draw the hot air out of the room; or a small circulating fan to cool everyone as they sat to listen to the radio after supper.

Chapter 7
Heard Street from Square, right side

Shell Filling Station operated by Mr. Charlie Bryant

The Shanty, originally owned by Denver Patterson, was located in parking area of station. It was later owned by Mr. and Mrs. Jack Bradford.

Colonial Grocery occupied large building next.

Scarborough's Pharmacy was next door, after moving off McIntosh Street.

Bluebird Hat Shop, run by McWhorter sisters, occupied third section on left of building.

Parking lot

Woodson's Florist, telephone #483, was located in small building where FBC Fellowship Hall now is. Prior to being Woodson's, it was named City Market. Later a new building was built on that spot and was occupied by Sears. It was later purchased by First Baptist.

Next was wooden two story FBC pastorium which sat where current FBC sanctuary sits.

Next, First Baptist Church at 132 Heard Street on corner of Heard Street and Thomas Street.

Heard Street from Square, left side

Patz and Fortson's on corner large retail clothing store. Attached was a small store that Mr. Henry Thomason occupied as a grocery store. Later was gift store of Fortson's. Much later, "The Scoop" ice cream parlor. Presently Phil Johnson's Insurance office is there.

Across from The Shanty was a three story rental house. It has been demolished and currently the location stands as Swift Park with Public Parking behind.

Southern Bell Telephone Office, 115 Heard Street, where telephone operators worked who were necessary for making a call, was located next. Building is now occupied by Steve Jenkins Law Office.

Remember "Number please?" That was before telephones had the dial system which is out of date now! Then, you picked up the telephone receiver and the operator – Bobbi Bagwell, Lorenne Brown, Frances Davis, Martha Fowler or Doris Webb, would ask that question before connecting you to the number you indicated to be called. Telephone Directory for Elberton and Royston, 1955, had numbers as:

Tony Campos #528-R and F. A. Johnson #1543. Residences that had only a number showed that it was a single party line. If the telephone number was followed by an alphabetical letter it mean that it was a party line that served two families. Numbers for separate houses were 528-J or 528-R. The family would know if the call was for them by hearing the ring as, one long ring meant the first family, two short rings meant the second family.

Some phone numbers were listed as 1794-W-3 or, 1168-R-7, which showed that they were three, and sometimes up to eight, residences on the same line. Many of these were to rural customers as those customers had to pay a mileage charge for the right to use the line. There were problems with families "listening in" on calls when the ring was not the one designated for their family. And, sometime if you needed to make a call and a member of the other party was on the line, you could "nicely" ask them for use of the line but, I've heard some were not so nice at that request!

In September, 1961, the new telephone office was opened on North Oliver Street and it was then that each home had a phone on which they dialed the party to whom they wished to speak. That was when 283-was placed before each number. What year was 213 added?

Lorene Brown remembers that she was classified as "the voice with a smile" when dialing went into effect and it was her voice you heard saying "hang up, you have dialed the wrong number."

143 Heard Street (this is address in 1956 telephone book) was location of Jones Appliance Maytag where home appliances could be purchased.

121 Heard Street (this is address in 1956 telephone book) was Bowers Furniture Store. Later Granite City Bank later used as bank offices.

GCB purchased lot of Fortson home and built a new bank. This was later purchased and Regions Bank now occupies that spot.

At one time ('54-'55) Palace Restaurant was run by Mr. and Mrs. W C. Beauford in next building

Next, was Moore's Cadillac Dealership, 139 Heard Street, across street from FBC pastorium.

These last two have been demolished and are now parking for FBC.

On corner was Dub Ayers Gulf Filling Station now occupied by Callaway Insurance.

South Oliver from Square

Courthouse which had been erected in 1893-94. For a period of time the grounds were surrounded with wrought iron fencing and the city water tank, which was erected in 1907, was located over the drive on the left of courthouse. In 1947-48, after the tank was drained, Milton Butler, along with other city employees, climbed inside, chipped off the rust and repainted it.

County Jail – Sheriff Adger Moore and family lived in front rooms, upper and lower levels. Did earlier sheriff families live there also? Presently is Jim Ree Museum.

S. Oliver Street left, behind Samuel Elbert Hotel

There was a white house with porch all around where John Harris and Judy Bailey lived. Later a taxi service ran from there run by Joe and Hazel Raynor. Ramona Gulley was dispatcher.

W. Church Street from South Oliver, right

Office Building where DFACS was located, now houses Action, Inc.

Photographer Everett Saggus had a studio in the house at 16 West Church, telephone #54, and Mary Alice (Smith) Bennett worked there.

Next was duplex home of Mr. and Mrs. W. W. Ellison (there was a large juke box on their back porch); and of Mrs. Williford (Bob and Billy's mother).

Leonard E. Hill home was next.

These last three have been demolished and Elbert County Detention Center was built there.

Granite Bowl

W. Church Street from South Oliver, left

Elbert Movie Theater, owned by Mr. Latimer Heard faced South Oliver. It is now home of Encore Productions which produces live plays at least four times a year and shows new movies intermittently.

McLanahan Chevrolet, telephone #26, owned by John W. McLanahan and run by his son Zack. Billy Webb was Service Manager with Billy Stratton and Cecil Bond working with him. Now Elbert County Community Service Center is at this address of 10 West Church Street

Elbert Health Department empty building

Hugh Wilhite home

Church Street, left from South Oliver

8 Church Street Service Cab Co. Telephone #67 "Fast, Dependable Service" advertisement.

Building 9 Church Street is now empty.

Jim Bradley Buick dealership was at 11 Church Street, left side, where Precision Fabrication is now located.

17 East Church served as Greyhound Bus Station, Ralph Rice's Auto Parts and now Robert Johnson's Law office. In the 1950s Mrs. Edna Mae Christie ran a school for tap and ballet upstairs.

Across McIntosh Street Arnold's Warehouse was located in large building corner where Ed Shive later had tire storage. Currently

Savannah Lakes Land Surveying Co. and Home, Sweet Home occupy the building.

Jules Fortson's Plumbing occupied the first store where Woodman's Life and Harper's Cleaning are presently.

Daisy's Beauty Shop occupied the next building where now Pam Brown's Insurance is located. Owner Daisy Middleton lived upstairs.

Elberton Milk and Ice Cream was next at 113 Church Street, run by Searcy and Lutz families. "Milk Ice Cream Whipping Cream Dairy Products Home Delivery" was advertisement.

There was an ice house next door and from there they delivered ice to individual homes which had "ice boxes" before electric refrigerators were standard.

Behind the ice cream parlor and ice house there was an open lot where WSB Radio personalities came for shows and where local carnivals took place.

A "Quonset Hut" rounded tin building next was the location of Wells Insurance.

In 1938 Anderson Auto Parts opened their first store on the next lot.

Next is the ROCK of First Baptist Church.

Do you remember when large oak trees grew in a middle section of Church Street in front of First Methodist Church/library/Cleveland home and the city use to hold public skating parties there? These trees were cut down but you can still see where the trees were located by the cuts in the paving.

Church Street, right from South Oliver

Whose home was located where Elberton Savings and Loan now stands?

Walton's Garage was at 12 West Church Street, tele. #785, where Norman Automotive is presently located.

Filling station corner Church and South McIntosh. This business had originally been Auld's Buggy and Bicycle Shop. In early 50's there was still one of the early buggies; and an old bicycle behind the wash rack per Bill Yarbrough. For a period of time this served as stopping point for Greyhound and Trailways busses.

House on corner facing South McIntosh Street Later demolished and Colonial Store occupied space where Cheap Deals Bargain Bazaar is presently.

Home of Elberton Police Chief Hugh Cleveland was on right side of Church Street. It had a large gold-fish pond in front yard.

Harris-Allen Library was located next in building built in 1891, as a library with Masonic/Eastern Star meeting space upstairs. It is presently owned by First Methodist Church and named the Bozeman Building. Miss Pauline Brewer Brown was librarian at one time.

On corner of Church and Thomas is First Methodist Church. The church was originally built of locally manufactured bricks. Because of storm damage in 1908/09 the brick was stuccoed over.

Chapter 8
Car Dealerships in Elberton

In the 1956 Southern Bell Telephone and Telegraph Company book there are listed nine new car dealerships within the city limits of Elberton. Today there are none.

The listings begin with Bradley Buick Company at 11 E. Church Street, telephone #749. This is the location where Precision Fabrication now stands. Mr. James Bradley who was assisted by his son James Louie owned this company. The company kept several new cars in stock but would order one to your specifications and it would be here within a week. Their logo printed in the book is "When Better Automobiles Are Built Buick Will Build Them."

Second listed is Brooks Motors on East Heard Street, telephone #659. They were "Packard Authorized Sales and Service." Their ad states "Ask The Man Who Owns One." Brothers Carl, Ralph and Harold (Hoss) Brooks owned this company. Its original location was where Oglesby and Son Garage is at 511 Elbert Street they built A new building on Williams Street and it is the building where "Scratch and Dent" is now located. Edgar Anderson and Travis Andrews worked in the body shop and all the Brooks brothers served as mechanics.

Third was Cadillac and Oldsmobile Sales and Service, 139 Heard Street, telephone 349, owned by Mr. Lowrey Moore. Cadillac logo was "Standard of the World" and Oldsmobile's was "Rocket! Hydra-Matic! Oldsmobile Has Both." This building has been demolished, but it stood where the parking lot is in front of First Baptist Church. Tom Brown, Joe Tom McMullan, James Atkins and Hugh Merritt were mechanics there and body workers were Bill Rosser and Gaines Driver.

Fourth was McLanahan Chevrolet Company at 17 W. Church Street, #26. This is the same building where "Elberton Art Center" is now located. "More people drive Chevrolets than any other car! More value... what's why!" states their logo. The company was owned by Mr. John McLanahan and was operated by his son, Zach McLanahan. Employees were Billy Webb, Billy Stratton, Pete Anderson and Al McKinney. Mr. Jack Bell handled their financial dealings. In years previous to the 1950s, Mr. Ben Sutton owned the Chevrolet dealership and occupied the space where the now closed office of Ed Shive Tire is located.

Fifth was Ray Auto owned by Mr. Will Ray. His business was at 126 N. Oliver, telephone #174. The company handled Chrysler-Plymouth automobiles and later, Allis Chalmers Tractors. Several members of the Ray family worked there - Estee Kellum and Roy Bert Ray were mechanics; Bodie Jones handled parts and Fred Ray and Bobby Ray were salesmen.

Mr. Will Ray and Mr. Claude Ray, Sr. were brothers and were in business together for a time. Mr. Will's grandson, Don Kellum, has a picture of the two of them standing in front of the Ray Motor Company.

Sixth. Dean Motor Company came next at 117 Heard Street, telephone #1240. They advertised "Dodge-Plymouth Dependable Service." Mr. Bobby Dean owned this dealership. Their sales room and car display faced Heard Street and its service department was in the basement where Wright's Automotive stands.

Seventh was Ford Authorized Sales and Service. It was located at 127 N. Oliver Street and was owned and operated by Mr. Claude

Ray with his two sons Claude, Jr. and Henry Doyle. The building has been demolished but stood where the N. Oliver exit to Walgreens and Pinnacle Bank is presently. "Bring Your Ford Back Home for Service" stated their logo. Mac Oglesby and Hubert West were two of their shop workers.

Eighth is Edwards Motor Company at 31 College Avenue, telephone # 630 for Mercury Sales and Service. "The Big M" ad was "Fully trained sales and service personnel, plus modern facilities and newest factory approved equipment for your convenience and satisfaction." Brothers, John Tom and Joe Edwards owned this. At one time they also handled Studebaker and Kaiser Frazier automobiles. Their service department was also located in their basement and employees were James Lunsford and Raymond Chandler.

Number Nine is Walton-Gaines Motor Company Pontiac Sales and Service at 15 College Ave., telephone #74 "Where To Buy Them" "Styled and Powered to Stay New For Years" were their ad logos. Mr. Henry Walton and Mr. Gene Gaines owned this company. Its address was 15 College Avenue which is the first building facing College Avenue heading north from Oliver Street. Employees were Frank Massey, Pete Anderson, Mac Oglesby, Pressley Baskin and Cecil Bond. Joe Carithers was the glass worker in the shop and when called upon, drove the wrecker. Bookkeepers were Manuel Fernandez and Chester Almond.

This building started out as a mule barn. Pete Anderson tells that when he worked there they stored large parts in the attic. When one such a part was needed, and you climbed the ladder to reach where they were stored, you also found bales of hay that had been left behind.

Needless to say I did not have personal knowledge of the above information. I had much fun listening to the many tales told by Norris (Pete) Anderson, Cecil Bond and Don Kellum. I am sure some worker names were left out. As you know the memories of 76, 78 and 82-year-old man are not what they used to be.

Chapter 9
Elberton's Service Stations

Do you *remember* 'gas' stations, 'filling' stations, 'service' stations? No matter which name you used it was THE place you had to return to with your automobile every time your gas register reached towards empty.

When you drove your car up to the gas pumps out front, a serviceman, note it was not a servicewoman, came up to your window and asked "Fill her up?" You then told him whether you wanted the tank filled with gas or you wanted $2, $5 or $10 worth of gas placed in the cars' tank. I remember that sometimes you got only $2 worth (today $2 wouldn't even buy one gallon) for if the price of the gas was $.50 a gallon then you would get 4 gallons. If your car traveled 20 miles on a gallon, then you could go 80 miles before needing additional gas. That would mean it was a week's worth of gas for you traveling to work and in/around town.

In additional to placing gas in the tank the serviceman would clean your windshield, check the oil, check the tires for amount of air and check any other item you asked for on your car. And they did all this for the price you paid for a gas fill-up! Oh, for the olden times!

Following are the names of most of the "filling" stations that were in Elberton during the fifties.

Beacon, phone #9137, later changed to Anchor Oil was on the Calhoun Falls Highway located where the VFW now stands. *"24 Hour Service Quality Gas–Diesel Fuel"* stated their ad.

Auld Brothers was at 106 S. McIntosh Street, Telephone #36. The building had been a carriage/buggy shop operated by earlier members of the Auld family. It later became Elberton's *Trailways/Greyhound* bus station.

Ayers Service was across the street from First Baptist Church where Callaway Insurance is now located. Dub Ayers operated this.

Mr. James Brewer (Mr. Jim) was owner, and his son Phil Tate, was the first operator, followed by Ralph Maxwell, then Gene Cornell in the station on the corner where Railroad Street and College Avenue came together just outside the city limits. Mr. Maxwell began operating at a new Phillips 66 station on College Avenue where James Car Wash is now located.

James Brown, with the help of Dub Ayers, operated a Gulf station at 143 Heard Street, telephone #9133. *"We pick up and deliver"* was their ad. He later moved to 570 Heard Street, selling Shell gasoline.

James Adams ran a station at 143 Heard Street, occupying the spot where Pizza Hut is located. James Lovinggood worked there. Mr. Adams sold the station and opened Elberton Motor Supply in the spot near the small city park and the parking lot for the high school gym is now on College Avenue.

Jimmy Gunnells and Fred Butler re-opened the station at 143 Heard, telephone #9147, selling Sinclair Gas. *"Always Courteous Service"* was their logo.

Charlie Bryant opened a Shell station, telephone #96 in the building where the Elberton Chamber of Commerce is now. For a time this station also served as the Trailways/Greyhound bus stop.

D C. Richardson operated the Granite City station, telephone #9134, located at 211 N. Oliver, at the corner of N. Oliver and Railroad Street.

V. G. Herring built a Standard station at the division of Heard and Elbert Streets. Marshall Sanders who sold Chevron Gas later purchased this station.

Mr. Sanders later purchased the station where Nava Tires is now located. He sold Sinclair Gasoline.

Herring Standard Service, operated by brothers, V.G., Jesse and Herman Herring, was at 16 College Avenue, telephone #461. This was later operated by brothers James H. and Harley Thomason then later it was operated by Pete and Lanier Anderson who sold Chevron gasoline at the same building.

George T Hewell operated City Service at the corner of Heard and Mill Streets. Telephone was #9113. He later sold Amoco gasoline.

McLanahan & Son, operated by Ben Senior and Ben Junior McLanahan sold Sinclair Gasoline on the corner of Oliver and Elbert Streets before Elbert Street was widened. Mr. McLanahan's son Hugh, delivered Atlanta Journal newspapers. The papers were delivered to him in the room that he used in the back of the station, or he traveled to Athens to pick them up.

Jule Parham operated Parham's Texaco on the corner of Heard and Williams Streets. Their telephone number was 595-J. *"Washing – Polishing – Lubricating – Waxing – We Call For and Deliver Your Car."*

Shell Service was at 21 College Avenue operated by Starke Hudson. Telephone # 9104. This was located on the left of the alley running from College Avenue to behind the court house. This was a meeting place for high school boys before they went to class in Central School up the street.

Toney's Pure Station was at 255 College, telephone #9131, was operated by Geek Clark who had a collection of Kaiser Frazier

Automobiles and a gun collection of more than 300 pistols which was stolen.

Frank Whitakers Service Station was originally at the corner of N. McIntosh and Deadwyler Streets. They sold Cities Service and when it moved to N. Oliver Street it changed to Texaco. Telephone was #3. This station was sold to Cecil Bond and operated as Rode Way Service. They serviced cars and were the only place in town for washing/servicing of 18 wheelers. The huge lot behind the station was a parking lot for trucks when they were not on the road. M & M Tire and Auto Care occupies this building now.

Mr. Clyde Brown was owner of the Gulf Station that was on the corner of N. Oliver and College Avenue, where Walgreens is now located. I lived on N. Oliver and walked, with friends, to Central school in the second through the fifth grades and on days it was warm we walked through the wash area of this station –in on College Avenue – out on N. Oliver. We thought it was so much cooler inside. Mr. D. C. Richardson operated this station for a time, then Mr. Ben and Zack McLanahan.

White's Gulf, operated by David White was at 142 N. Oliver, Telephone #9130, where J and D Auto Repair is. Coy Attaway was the attendant there who later moved to Whitaker's then Rode Way Service.

Broadus West operated an Amoco Station on N. Oliver in the building occupied by J and D Auto Repair.

Melanie B. Childs remembered a small service station at the intersection of Highways 17 and 72, before the highways were widened. Another person said that Mr. Floyd Dye ran it.

As you have read through this, you notice the same attendants at different 'filling' stations. It seems that this was a great work experience to some men and they moved around as situations or owners changed.

Today not one station in Elberton offers a similar service. Now you drive up to the tanks outside a convenience store and pump your own gas. There is no "charge it," you either pay cash or use a credit card. That has been a new experience for some, particularly women who had never pumped gas for their cars. It is true for me as I had never pumped gas in the 18 years my husband had a station. After selling the station, the pickup was his, and the car was mine and if the car needed gas, I had to pump it.

You may find that we left out, or didn't have the correct information in some instances, but I thank Pete Anderson and Cecil Bond for their many remembrances that made this article possible.

Do You Remember When

Your bedroom, which was NOT heated, was so cold that your mother placed so many quilts on the bed you could hardly turn over.

Chapter 10
Old Time Businesses

Before the current "Magic Market's" and "Mister B's" type convenience stores, there were many small stores located in the residential areas around town.

Mr. Henry Thomason's at 252 North Oliver Street.

Mrs. McConnell's at 313 North Oliver Street, just above Tate Street. It was owned by Jessie Miller. You could call in an order, it would be filled and then delivered by a boy on a bike. Mrs. McConnell and Mrs. Miller lived in the house next door, 313 North Oliver Street.

Cleveland's, on Tate Street, owned by Cleveland.

Duncan's Grocery at 240 Highland Drive.

Mr. Hubert Stalnaker's on the corner of Laurel Drive and College Avenue.

Mr. Henry Fowler's Grocery and Repair Shop on the corner of Edwards and Tusten Streets.

Bob Roberts first, then Herman Barton, ran a store on the corner of Adams and South McIntosh Streets.

Jolly John's, owned by Mr. John C. Fortson, then Mr. Joe Christian, on the right of College Avenue at College Avenue Extended.

Ideal Grocery, owned by Mr. Claude Barger 333, College Avenue.

Otis Callaway's where Tractor Supply now stands.

A store at 370 Cleveland Street run by Mr. Tom Hewell.

A store on the corner of Gordan and Parker Streets owned by Jesse Mae Hall.

Thornton's Grocery, on the right of Gordon Street, owned by Oscar Thornton. Carol Gunter Walters said that she went to Thornton's after school one day and found Mr. Thornton deceased but still sitting in a chair. Carol's mother Mrs. Zeke (Mazelle) Gunter, who was an employee there, bought the store from Mr. Thornton's wife and later sold it to Mr. George Bettis.

On Gordon Street, at the sharp turn towards the city quarry, was a store first owned by Seab McGarity then later by James Lunsford.

Another store, not named, come on dammit but the building still stands on South Oliver across from the building where Not Just Dolls was located.

On Lake Forest Drive was a store run by Mr. Carithers.

William's Store, on the corner of South Oliver and Adams Streets; it had wooden benches outside.

At the West End Grocery, owned by Bert Barger on the corner of College Avenue and Worley Street, 'Uncle Homer' Vaughn was the head of the meat market where all the meat was fresh cut and wrapped as ordered, and he would 'check your oil' on kids by pinching their fanny! Your groceries could be called in and whoever answered the phone would write down your order, then get a cart and begin filling your order. R. D. Holland was the deliveryman. Marco Goodwin worked there along with part-time help Marion Fortson (Fortson and Sanders, CPA), Donald Hulme, Parker Dixon, Bill Yarbrough and George Ward, (later police chief). My family did not have a car so my mother, Mrs. F. A. Johnson, always bought groceries there since the store delivered at no extra cost. Many years later when our son, Mark, was born and weighing only four pounds eight ounces when he left the hospital, we took him to West End once a week for several weeks and Uncle Homer weighed him on the meat scale.

Z. W. Copeland's Grocery was a wholesale warehouse for all types of goods including grocery, animal feed and tobacco products. Salesmen (Mr. Newt Acker, Nathan's father, was one) traveled to country stores along Washington Highway. Then to Tignall, Palmetto, Rayle, Lexington, Enterprise, and others, taking orders and returning on Lexington Highway. He turned the orders in and the next day they were delivered by truck. The next day salesmen went to Goss, Dewy Rose, Bowman, Vanna, Royston, 13 Forks, etc. They turned in orders and the next day the ordered items were delivered. This process was repeated until areas, in several counties by several salesmen, some even into South Carolina were covered. I remember going in that huge building–so cool, it smelled so good–coffee beans, spices, candy. I went there with my daddy, F. A. Johnson, for him to purchase Copenhagen. It was located at 139 North Oliver but the building was demolished in the fall of 2011. Dennis Gunter remembers going there after his paper route to buy penny candy with the money he had earned.

The Coca Cola Bottling Company Plant, telephone #125, which is located at the intersection of Elbert, Locklin and Heard Streets, was built in 1928 by Mr. H. J. Miller, father of Harry Miller. Mr. H. J. Miller had Coca Cola plants in Augusta and Waynesboro with a partner. This partner was on the Standardization Committee of Coca Cola to standardize future plants to be built by the company. The Elberton plant is the first built under the newly adopted standard that included putting the Coca Cola logo, emblazoned in cement, across the front of the building.

Mr. Harry Miller began operating the Elberton plant in 1946. The plant received the syrup, used in processing, in 50-gallon stainless steel drums. It was mixed, one-ounce syrup to five and a half ounces of carbonated water and poured into the familiar six and a half ounce *hobble-skirt* coke bottles.

Each year Mr. Miller and employees made trips to each elementary school passing out pencils, tablets and rulers. Many classes came to visit the plant and on their return, the letters of appreciation always mentioned the round metal stairway from the ground to the second floor. This stairway could be seen through the large glass window on the front of the building.

The building is currently occupied by Safehouse Ministries.

Argo Trucking Company, East Heard Street, telephone #957. The owner was Mr. Grady Albertson, and the company ran a fleet of trucks that hauled granite all over the U.S. Mr. Albertson had quarried the granite obelisk, similar to the Washington Monument, that is now located behind the EGA office.

In the early 1900s the area around the square, South McIntosh to Adams Street, North McIntosh to Deadwyler, North Oliver to the railroad crossing, portions of Railroad Street, to the Oil Mill; Deadwyler Street in front of the railroad depot, College Avenue to the Comolli Home (where The Medical Center is located now); were paved with brick, cobble stones or paving blocks. I've not identified additional streets that were bricked. I questioned from where these paving materials were purchased, and who did the work of laying all these areas? And, if part of it had been cut to brick size from granite, who cut and furnished it?

The alley behind the Poole Building still has a small amount of brick paving that has not been covered. The alley was nicknamed "Ambulance Alley" because the Elberton Hospital was on the third floor, above the First National Bank, (now the Poole Building). As ambulances brought patients to the hospital, they drove into the alley where a street level door was opened for the patient to be carried inside to an elevator which then delivered the patient to the hospital floor.

If you go to the children's play area of M. J. Sutton Park off Forest Avenue, you will see the creek that runs through it lined, for 40-50 feet on both sides, with rocks. Mr. Ben Sutton owned that land, and he proposed to erect a house there that straddled the branch. Niles Poole and Nathan Acker both stated that Mr. Sutton had rocks placed there in preparation for his proposed home. But he never built on that site.

There was a Southern Railroad engine turnaround located at the corner of Railroad and North Oliver Streets. Because locomotives of the era could not go in reverse, the engine had to be turned around to enable it to push the cars on the return to Toccoa. The Southern Freight Depot is still standing on Railroad Street just to the left of the turnaround. In talking with several people it has been said that there was also a Passenger Depot located to the right of the Freight Depot. There are spots of paving in several locations where the Passenger Depot stood. If you go to the Freight Depot and walk the area, you can see the cross-ties, now almost covered in dirt that held the rails on which the train traveled. The Freight Depot's location is shown on the 1922 Sanborn Insurance maps.

When they were children, Jeanne (Clinkscales) Phelps, who lived at 251 North Oliver Street, and Barbara Hammond who lived at 135 North Oliver were, at different times, invited to ride as the engine turned around.

Once a small wooden building, used as a Boy Scout meeting place, was on the left of Lake Forest Drive heading toward the city lake. Another Boy Scout meeting cabin was located beside the tennis courts that were on Heard Drive.

The first Knox (company name) home built in Elberton is located at the corner of North Oliver and East Tate Street beside former home of Dr. D. V. Bailey. In 1949, 50 and 51 many Knox prefabricated homes were built on Lake Forest Drive, Brookhaven and Cactus Hill Drive.

Why were the large buildings on North McIntosh, behind Bojangles, built? Dennis Gunter said the first one stored cotton bales and second one was a warehouse for the Elberton Compress.

One is constructed of pieces of granite shaped and sized like a brick. Where did these granite pieces originate? They do not have a smooth finish, so they were not sawed. Are they similar to ones used in original paving of streets?

The building at 244 New Street, formally beside those listed, has been demolished. It also had an advertisement for "Million Chew." I haven't found the name of the product for which this advertisement was printed.

Immediately behind the Old City Hall on North McIntosh Street was another building that had painted on one side "Moore's Garage." I learned that Red McCullough had machine shop there where he rebuilt motors, and it once was a blacksmith shop run by Tom Gunter. The Old City Hall, on North McIntosh and "Moore's Garage" on New Street were torn down in the spring of 2009.

There are two buildings behind 31 College Avenue. One is about 40 by 80, and the second is much smaller and its roof has fallen in. Both have "For Sale" signs painted on them and one has "Firestone" painted on the outside. For what were these used, and who are the owners?

When talking with Shirley McNeely she remembers living on South McIntosh Street, and as a child she rode her bike, or skated, up the street to Auld's Station and they would "oil" her skates or place air in a bicycle tires.

Mr. Quinn Wansley had his home and ran a junkyard at 149 Railroad Street, telephone #908. He had car parts, granite industry parts, any type of metal parts and other miscellaneous items, spread over his yard. His premises were located where Granite Sales & Supply and EGA offices currently stand. There was no street from Railroad Street to College Avenue then, since his yard involved all that space.

The town trash dump, which was burned daily, was located on the back side of Elmhurst Cemetery in area that is now the "new" portion of cemetery. The area was cleared of burned rubbish before being made part of cemetery. The trash dump area went down to fenced area at rear of present cemetery.

Chapter 11
Colorful Places and Events

A lady contacted me saying her father took their family to the square to see the hypnotized lady in the Gallant Belk's window; she *thought* her name was Smith. I was stopped on the square by a lady that said she remembered the lady being hypnotized and she *thought* her last name was Berryman. Barbara Hammond furnished, with certainty, the information that it was Mrs. Alma Autry that was hypnotized and spent the afternoon in Belk's window. Mrs. Autry was transported by ambulance to the place where the hypnotist's show was to be held. Barbara did not attend so she does not know the show's location.

In a letter from former resident of Elbert County's Fortsonia Community, George W. Bell, said, "The lady's name was indeed Mrs. Alma Autry. She was "put under" as a stunt that advertised and led up to an evening entertainment event that night at the Elberton Armory Auditorium. Mrs. Autry was hypnotized during the late morning and transported to the window of Belk's by an ambulance owned by T. M. Martin Funeral Home. During Mrs. Autry's slumber, a local dentist extracted a tooth or two that Mrs. Autry wanted yanked. She was not to have been awakened until her arrival on stage as the last act of the show. This was not to be. The ambulance attendants could not get her, and the gurney, out of the narrow door to the window of Belk's when the proper time came. Therefore, she had to be briefly awakened so as to be allowed to walk out of the window area and then be hypnotized again and carried to the arena. This was never announced." Mr. Bell did not tell how she was awakened, then put back to sleep.

Remember the Drive-in Movie that was on the lot where Ingle's now stands? Mrs. Pete (Mattie) Tate ran the stand where you could purchase colas, popcorn, crackers and candy. In the Elberton City Directory 1966-67, her job title was Concessionist.

The city lake was located between Lake Forest Drive and Brookhaven. It was filled by a creek that runs from the original Elbert County Spring which is under the Granite Bowl, and a creek that runs through Sutton Park. The lake had a section roped off for swimming with a diving platform but the area was closed after a local youth drowned there.

Once there was a swimming pool located just inside the city limits on the left of North Oliver at the immediate right of Veteran's Park. According to his daughter, Iris T. Anderson, Phil Tate, owned it. Although the pool was privately owned, it was open to the public. There was a dance hall beside the pool and Jack Ridgeway played piano there.

During the 1950s, Elberton had several temporary skating rinks. At various times they were located:

1) On the lot where the Dollar General now stands on Lower Heard Street. It was run by Ed and Helen Ayers.

2) On the lot behind the present Dairy Queen parking lot.

3) Beside the Lunsford's home on the Hartwell Highway.

4) According to Richard Rucker, one of the very earliest was located on the lot later occupied by Argo Trucking Company, on lower Heard Street.

5) On the Athens Highway, just beyond the overhead bridge was another early one.

Granite was used on the outside of the Catholic and Lutheran churches on Forest Avenue and the Episcopal Church on Brookside Drive. Marvin Hardy stated that the male members of the Episcopal Church laid the stone. The Episcopal Church began their meetings at the former Payton Hawes home on Heard Street and the local men of the Episcopal denomination built the church. The Lutheran Church originally met Sunday afternoons upstairs in the former Library and Masonic Hall on Church Street with a minister from Newberry South Carolina leading the services.

There was once a *movie* made of Elberton kids. Dr. and Mrs. D. V. Bailey lived down North Oliver from me and their grandchildren, Jane and Bob. Mrs. Bailey took the three of us to "registration and try-outs" that were held in the courtroom of the courthouse. When finished, the three of us went running out to the car (a navy blue Chrysler) parked in the parking lot behind the courthouse. When we saw Mrs. Bailey coming, we ducked down into the floorboard where she couldn't see us. She thought we weren't in the car and went all the way back upstairs looking for us. There was NO elevator back then; needless to say, we were *talked to,* when she got back to the car.

Peggy Galis said that the movie was a project of the Logan-Jenkins Company who owned the local movie theater. It was made for the promotion of the theater and Elberton. What happened to the movie? Did anyone ever see it?

Once a woman came to town pushing a wheelbarrow. She was walking from Florida up the east coast. She stayed at Samuel Elbert Hotel and everyone went to see her.

Marvin Hardy remembers the "Goat Man" coming through town with 6-8 goats pulling a wagon. He was traveling across country, sleeping in a tent each night. As people gathered round, he milked the goats and drank the milk.

Marvin Hardy Jr., called and told that he used to ride his bike to Mrs. A. C. (Acie) Rousey's home, behind 259 North Oliver Street, for her to take care of alterations to items customers purchased at Poole's Men's Store.

Marvin also remembered Shirley (Shell) McNeely playing a special part for the piccolo in "Stars and Stripes Forever" when performed by the Elberton High School band. He said that many years later when he was at a concert by the Boston Pops Orchestra, and they began playing that song, he could hardly wait to hear the piccolo part– but, unfortunately, that part was not included in their orchestration of the song. "In 2014 I watched the July 4th program of music and fireworks from Washington, DC and the orchestra played 'Stars and Stripes Forever' and the piccolo part was excellent!"

Bill Yarbrough said that a Boy Scout troop met in the basement of the First National Bank (Poole Building). It had double doors which opened into "Ambulance Alley," the same door used by ambulances, and the troop walked along the long hall and met in a large room on the left near the front of the building basement. The Scoutmaster was Stuart Lyle.

Marvin Hardy said that his brother-in-law, H. M. Williams, met weekly with a group to play table tennis (ping-pong) in the same downstairs area. He supposed that the table is still there.

Remember when Elberton had a baseball team? It was "king' in Elberton in early 1900s-1940s.

One game, possibly played in 1948, had Elberton playing Calhoun Falls. "Tuffy" Embler was playing 2nd base and Albert Brown was batting for Elberton. Albert hit a "mile high" ball over 2nd base and Tuffy lost it in the lights. He circled around under it trying to find it and the ball finally hit behind his back. The crowd screamed at the 2nd baseman and Tony Campos came running out from the bleachers, crossed the base line going to the 2nd baseman and handed Tuffy a "peach basket" for him to catch the next ball in. The crowd roared.

In the early 1920s when the City of Elberton joined the "Million Dollar League" the crowds would total close to 1000 per game.

The pride and joy of the Elberton community was their semi-professional baseball team and the well maintained ballpark, with grandstand and bleachers, which was located on North McIntosh Street Night baseball started in 1938 when the WPA put up park lights for the City of Elberton and prepared the five acre Elberton Athletic Field at the North McIntosh Street location

Elberton's teams had various names over the years – Peaches, Blue Sox, Cardinals; and they played in various leagues – The Million Dollar League and Georgia-Carolina League among them.

Players listed in 1940 were: Smith(p), Russ Lyons(c), Jenkins(lf), Ben Brown (ss), Herndon (cf) Watt Cooley (p and 1b), Lee (lf), Gudger Kirkland (rf), Killands (1b) Eddie Frank Craft (p), Leo Wilson (2b), Hansard (p), Clyde Hewell (3b), Smith (p), McCaskill (p). (From Larry Wilson)

Remember Stoney Williams? He was in his 20s or 30s and became the mascot for the Elberton Blue Devils. He was mentally slow but loved any high school sport, especially football. He was always taken to out-of-town games. He was given a football jacket that he wore on every occasion possible. On Sunday's he would always attend church at First Baptist. He came in carrying his tie and asked one of the men to tie it for him. He lived in the house on the left corner of South Oliver and Lake Forest Streets.

Remember "Crazy Mary"? She was a black lady who walked all over town. She never hurt anyone and took any handout of food or money. It was said that she was sitting on the porch rocking her baby girl and lighting struck killing the baby causing her mind to snap.

Remember when the Spencer Taylor band, all local musicians, was much the rage and was called on to perform at many events?

Do you remember when all Elbert County vehicle tags were 50-XYZ? The 50 designated the fact that Elbert County was ranked 50th in population in Georgia. A few years later, it was changed to 51 for the same designation. Do you remember which years those tags came out? Do you happen to have kept one? Do you realize that according to the 2010 census that Elbert County is now ranked 90th in Georgia population?

The "Silver Comet" the passenger train of the Seaboard Coastline Railroad came through Elberton twice each day. When I was 12 years old, I visited cousins in DC and I traveled by myself back to Elberton on the Comet. Because of safety concerns, this would not be allowed today.

I remember that families would gather to send a member on a trip and wait to hear the "All Aboard" from the Conductor as the train made ready to leave the station.

After the high school burned in 1955, high school students attended classes in the First Methodist and First Baptist churches, which are only one block apart. When junior Carole Albertson turned 16, her parents gave her a turquoise and white Metropolitan to drive. If you remember Metropolitans, they were SMALL, smaller than a VW. I was told that one day a group of male students picked up her car from its parking spot on Church Street and placed it in an area between the Methodist church building and its shrubbery. The male who told me this said, "THEY picked it up, and I just watched."

Back in the 1950s, mail delivery was very different. Mr. Ping Johnson was our mailman to North Oliver Street and he walked his route every day having a large leather bag over his shoulder that contained mail for North Oliver, and connecting side streets. And he knew the patrons on his route. We once received a letter from out of town addressed:

TO: The Shine Johnsons

All Sizes and Sex

Elberton GA

Donnie Matthew tells that in 1957, when he was 16, his dad gave him a 1947 Ford. But, his dad kept a check on the car's mileage to make sure he was not *riding around* too much. Of course, Donnie didn't appreciate that, so he determined to seek a way to keep mileage from showing on the odometer. In the process, he found that if you drove the car backwards, the mileage would not register. So, late one afternoon, when neither of his parents was home, he drove his car BACKWARDS from his home on South Oliver, down Lake Forest Drive, around the lake coming out beside the Catholic Church. He then went up Forest Avenue, to College Avenue, then down to McDounough Street to pick his friend Donald Boswell. They continued out College onto the Athens Highway and stopped at the skating rink that was just past the overhead bridge. After skating a while, he drove home covering the same territory meaning that the mileage did not show on the odometer. He says his dad may have had suspicions, but he never discovered how Donnie had gotten past his requirements.

Do You Remember When

You or someone you knew, lived on a farm where sugar cane was grown and a mule was hitched up to go round and round grinding the cane? Then, grandpa cooked it into sorghum syrup to go on those delicious buttered biscuits.

Chapter 12
Elberton's Mills

The Elberton Cotton Mill Fabricated cotton cloth and Mr. W. D. Minter was the manager. Housing was built to house workers on Wilson, Cedar, Gordon, Parker, Atlantic, Tribble and Hamilton Streets.

After the mill closed the building was used for constructing travel trailers (RV's); then by George Goss, for Southernaire Construction operations. It presently serves as the Elbert County Recycling Center.

The Silk Mill was built in 1926 on Seaboard Street. Originally, it fabricated silk material. When built, it was the only mill of its kind in Southern United States because it made cloth from raw materials imported from China and Japan. Rental houses for the workers were built all around mill. The mill closed in 1939, but United Merchants purchased and began operations again in 1941. Mr. Dan McCanless was the manager in the 1950s. The rental houses were sold to the workers in the 1950s. Glen Raven purchased the mill in the 1980's. After Several years, they ceased operations. Demolition began in the fall of 2014. The main portion of the mill is still standing.

    The Elberton Rug Mill, on Railroad Street. Jonnie Roberts worked there 26 years, starting in 1943. Mr. Tom Colley was the owner and shortly after Jonnie went to work "he made her boss and put her in charge of everything." They made rugs, handmade plow lines to use with plowing mules, tarpaulin and combine sheets used to gather grain. They also sold piece goods. Jonnie went to Ft. Gordan and purchased second hand boots, fatigues, pants and shirts. These were sold primarily to granite workers.

    Kate Buchanan and Ida Sue Craft worked there in the plant. Pauline Rampey and Jimmie Cobo served as bookkeepers. (Jonnie Roberts)

    At an Army "buy out" sale Mr. Tom Colley purchased a small airplane which he piloted for several years. Later after landing at the local airport, then between Highway 72 West and Highway 17 South, he had the plane taken apart. Its parts were moved to his Rug Mill property and sold to individuals.

    There is a small cemetery at the rear section of the Rug Mill property.

    The Elberton Flour Mill, was built in 1941, by Bodie Anderson who never ran it. Brothers Ira and Glenn Ayers purchased it and began its operation in 1942. "Nancy Hart" was the brand name they gave to the cornmeal and flour they ground from local corn and wheat. They also made livestock feed. In 1948 Ira bought his brother's half and ran the mill by himself until 1974/76. (Ed Ayers)

The Oil Mill. Mr. W. O. Jones opened The Cotton & Compress Company, which became known locally as The Oil Mill, around 1890. It was at 62 Railroad Street, telephone #13, in 1956.

There were several buildings in the complex–the main one housed the manufacturing operation to collect the oil from cottonseeds, another manufactured soap and a third was the oil stand tank.

In 1907, the soap factory burned and was not replaced. In 1963 after being idle for several years, the other buildings burned. The "Historic Elberton" by Joyce M. Davis contains an outline drawing of all the facilities. Its location was where a saw shed and outside granite storage area is operated by Central Granite Company on Railroad Street.

In April 2014, I interviewed Mr. Donald Hudson who was 80 years of age; he stated that his uncle, Mr. Ward Bell, was the manager at the Oil Mill for many years. In March 2015, after publishing of the first article concerning The Oil Mill, Mr. George Bell of Atlanta contacted me and said that his father was the uncle spoken of by Mr. Donald Hudson and included additional information about The Oil Mill. Here I have combined the information from both, Mr. Hudson and Mr. Bell to provide more complete details concerning the Mill operation.

Mr. Hudson said his family had 100 acres, on the right of Highway 17 going toward Tignall, which they planted in cotton each year. At maturity, 40 black women from Washington, GA, came and picked it for them every year. Throughout the county, farmers weighed the cotton and paid the pickers, per pound, their due amount.

They loaded the loose cotton on trucks and covered it with sheets of fabric tied down so the cotton was completely enclosed. The trucks delivered it to the Oil Mill to be ginned. The Oil Mill ran two gin lines from daybreak to midnight during harvest time every day except Sunday, for Mr. Bell was at church on His day.

Mr. Hudson said they usually carried their cotton to the gin in the late afternoons and early evenings. He said that during cotton-picking season the yard of the Oil Mill would be covered with trucks and wagons loaded with cotton. Peggy H. Galis said that the first job of her father Robert M. Heard in the early 1920s, was to ride his pony around the mill yard dispensing numbers designating the order their load would be ginned.

The cotton brought from local farms was vacuumed from the trucks by a forced air dryer where every single drop of moisture evaporated from the raw cotton. All the extra weight went up in the air.

To "gin" meant that the cotton, after being dried, the seeds were separated from the lint by a series of mechanical *combs and brushes* that had been invented by Eli Whitney. This lint was then packed into burlap sheeting and strapped by metal bands into a cube shaped bale, five feet high with a four foot cross section weighing about 500 pounds. Mr. Hudson said they received a 500-pound cotton bale for every 1,200 pounds of seed cotton they took to the gin.

The value of a bale was determined by supply and demand, the weight and the *staple length*. Staple length referred to how long the single threads of lint averaged. The longer the staple, the greater the value. This lint was sold to be spun into thread and the thread woven into cloth.

The seeds removed from the cotton were not just used for planting next year's crop. Workers moved the seeds to another area in the complex where they were crushed, pressed and strained; the oil was then stored in the huge stand tank behind the mill. The oil was sold to large companies and transported as needed. Cottonseed oil had many uses, especially in the food industry. The two most noted uses of cotton seed oil from The Elberton Oil Mill were the major ingredient of Wesson Oil and a prime component of Duke's mayonnaise.

Only a small portion of cotton seeds processed by The Elberton Oil Mill were grown in Elbert County–the Mill sent buyers all over the Southeastern United States to buy cotton seed which was then trucked, or brought in, by rail.

The ground hulls of the cottonseeds were pressed into sheets and baked into *meal cake*; meal cake was ground into yellow meal to be used as livestock feed or as a compliment to mixed livestock feed. Baking the meal cake produced a delicious aroma. I know because I grew up on North Oliver Street where the back of our lot joined The Oil Mill property. One fall day the high school band of which I was a part, had after-school practice. A friend brought me home and when I opened the car door to get out he said, "Ooh, WHAT is your mother cooking for supper?"

Mr. Hudson said that he and his dad sometimes swapped seed cotton for the hulls and yellow meal to feed to their cows as roughage.

On the TV show "American Pickers" that was shown February 25, 2015, the men of the show were at Clinton, SC, and one picker pulled an item from a shelf, dusted it off and it was a thermometer with advertising on it for "Elberton Oil Mill Elberton, Georgia, Telephone #13." He purchased for $75 and valued it at $150.

Mr. Bell said that there was a wide variety of logo items: calendars, serving trays, pens, ash trays, farmer's wallets, bottle openers, writing pads, etc. Johnny Webb showed me a short pencil which has separate metal parts covering the head and the pencil lead and Ben Rice brought by a pocket knife; both have the Oil Mill logo on them.

Elberton Oil Mill's motto was: "A SATISFIED CUSTOMER IS OUR FIRST CONSIDERATION."

Do You Remember When

You had dresses and skirts your mother made from the sacks of feed or flour used at your house? Or maybe when you got to go to *the cloth store to* BUY material for the dresses your mother made for school.

Chapter 13
Seaboard Airline Railway Traveling Library

In 1898 Mrs. Eugene B. Heard, who had been born in Newton County, Georgia, lived with her husband at Rose Hill Plantation near Middleton, Georgia. Mrs. Sarah, or Sally as she preferred to be called, was a famous hostess in the area after she married Mr. Eugene who had inherited a 2,000 acre plantation given to one of his ancestors, Georgia's Gov. Stephen Heard. After their marriage they had a daughter Susan, and a son, Thomas. Books were birthday, Christmas and anytime gifts to both, but Thomas, more than Susan, spent much of his time enthralled in the stories he read. When he was about twelve an illness caused his sudden death. As he and Susan had a large collection of books, his mother, hoping to share those books and his love of reading, began to loan them to neighborhood children. Such a response she received! She found children and adults who were hungry for reading material so she began to loan books from Rose Hill's library collection. Then she began asking friends to donate books for this Cause. They did, but there still were not sufficient books for the requests. She was so thrilled at their response that she decided to do all she could to see that all rural people had access to books for their reading.

Mr. Everitte St. John, Vice-President of the Seaboard Airline Railway, was in Elberton, which was near Middleton, discussing expansion of the railway system. Hostess that she was, Mrs. Heard invited him to Rose Hill and while he was there she presented information to all present concerning the possibility of a library for everyone who lived along the length of the Seaboard Railway. This was news to him, but as Mr. St. John visited at Rose Hill for several days, he saw the children who came for books and recognized the need. Before he left her home, he offered the Seaboard Railway's services in distributing the books and his offer was for all the states in which the Seaboard system operated. He stated that it would be done IF Sally could get the books to the railway, then they would distribute them, FREE OF CHARGE, to any person or any community wherever the railroad ran.

The next step was to get books and more books, to get magazines and more magazines to fulfill the need. Sally Heard traveled up the East coast soliciting these texts from every publishing house and came home with promises of free books and magazines–promises that were kept long after her death.

Sally's next step was to arrange with communities along the Seaboard for handling circulation of the books. She again rode the Seaboard line from one end to the other traveling through all six states securing the cooperation of women in taking over the operation of the "circulating library" boxes.

In 1901, the newspaper *Salmagundi*, "Devoted to the Seaboard Air Line Railway and the Agricultural and Industrial Interests of the South," printed letters from U.S. President William McKinley, the Governors of all six Seaboard Railway states, Andrew Carnegie and others commending Sally on her noble work and pledging monies and their full support. Mr. G. R. Glenn, Georgia State School Superintendent wrote, "Nobody can estimate the value of good clean books placed in the hands of little children. Many of those precious little lives will date the beginning of new aspirations and new hope to the time when you placed these books in their hands."

Remember this began in 1898, and by 1912 fourteen years later, 18,000 books and 36,000 magazines were being distributed to individuals in these states!

Sally died in 1919, after spending all her days working tirelessly to promote and expand the Seaboard Airline Railway Traveling Free Library. At her death Sallie's daughter Susan assumed the role of head librarian and it was continually supported by women up and down the eastern seaboard and through continued donations from publishers and private citizens alike.

The library did not close until 1955, and by that time county, regional and state library programs had developed in each of the six states. As it closed all the remaining books were turned over to the Elberton schools.

The vision of one woman, Mrs. Sally Heard, came to fruition and the lives of thousands of men and women, boys and girls were enriched through the books that came to them from this unique library. In all its years of existence no fines were ever charged for overdue books, nor where there charges made for lost books. There were no regulations, no State aid, no Federal aid and no local funds. The librarians who donated their time for the operation of the library were neither trained nor certified, but their knowledge of books, love of people and devotion to a cause were as effective as any graduate library degree could have been. The standards of service were simple good will and a concern for others. Its history is a miracle which can be attributed to one woman's vision, the generosity of publishers, a level-headed businessman and the tracks of the Seaboard Railway System.

Works cited:

"So Good and Necessary a Work"   Estellene P. Walker

Story of the Seaboard Air Line Free Traveling Library   Mrs. James Y. Swift

Sarah Harper "Sallie" Heard   P. Toby Graham

"Books Ride the Rails in Unique Railroad Library"   Nell S. Graydon

In the early 1960s several of the community service clubs, especially the Elberton Civic League, became interested in fulfilling the need for better library service in Elbert County. It was learned that Elbert County was one of only three counties in the state having no county or regional service and therefore being ineligible to receive state aid.

In February 1967 a bond for $95,000 was voted on to erect a building for a new library on Heard Street property that had been donated by the B. F. Coggins Foundation. The state contributed matching building funds and the county and the city voted to each place $150.00 per month towards library support.

Contributions continued to be received throughout 1968, and the new facility was opened on April 4, 1969. Mrs. Frank Maxwell, who had formerly served at Harris Allen Library, Elberton, served as Director until June 1969 when Mr. William Muller took the position. He served until June 1972, and Mrs. Paula (Suddeth), now Bulloch, took the position in July of that year.

Mrs. Suddeth began using her personal vehicle as a "car-mobile" by delivering books to several county locations on a regular basis. A newspaper article in May 1976 stated: "We are going to get a bookmobile" and after many discussions, estimates and decisions, with federal help, a Ford van was purchased in October 1978. The van had an extended top with seating only in the front with the back area open for shelving to be installed that would hold books/magazines in place while traveling.

The opening set-up for bookmobile distribution, done on a monthly basis, was to: Ruckers's Store, Ruckersville; Powell's Store, Rock Branch; Adam's Store, Centerville; Page's Store, Clark's Junction; Rabbit Well; Rose Hill; Worley's Store; Rice's Store, Ricetown; Hudson's Store, Fortsonia; Oglesby's Store, Doves Creek; Parham's Store, Deep Creek; Segar's Store, Dewy Rose; City Hall,

Bowman; Fred Lewis Store, Fork Creek; Grimes Store, Indian Hill; and Whispering Pines Trailer Park. Mrs. Suddeth and Mrs. Anderson and Miss Nancy McCall served as drivers.

After 20 years of service and MANY miles, the "old" bookmobile was retired, donated to the county, and a new extended cab Ford was purchased in April 1998. It has already been driven 28,955 miles in support of reaching people who cannot make stops at the city library. Nancy McCall Mathews and Peggy J. Johnson continued as the assigned drivers and stops at Headstart, Child Development Center, nursing homes, several personal care homes, hospital, jail and Senior Center were incorporated along with several of the previous stops.

These bookmobiles, the second one now being driven by Rene McCollum, have carried on the services in Elbert County that the Seaboard Traveling Library had conveyed to the six states in which it traveled.

Currently, hard back and paperback books and magazines of recent issue are always accepted as donations and are especially used by the bookmobile.

Information received from Vertical Files of Elbert County Library

Do You Remember When

After the cows were milked, having to churn the milk, which took maybe 25 minutes but seeming like FOREVER, to make butter for those tasty biscuits; and buttermilk, in which you broke up cornbread for a delicious snack.

Chapter 14
Good Eating - Cafes Restaurants

Elberton had several cafes: The 72 Drive-In which was just past 'overhead bridge' on Athens Hwy. run by Pete Scales; a dance hall and café across from "Tate's Place" home, on Athens Highway; "The Green Lantern" on College Ave.(Owned by Phil Tate); "Red Hell" on S. Oliver Street; The Dew Drop In on Elbert Street; Crick's Place on N. McIntosh Street; Reagin's Grocery/Restaurant on Railroad Street across from Coggins Granite; and The Silver Grill on Lower Heard Street Several of these were shut down by county Grand Jury!

The Toot & 'Tellum restaurant was located in the fork of the road where Hwy. 17 and Hwy 72E met and its owner was Mr. Tom Burton. Do you remember "Tutter" Shell who worked there? Tutter was Tom's sister-in-law and mother of Shirley S. McNeely. The restaurant later moved to left side Hwy. 72E and renamed "The Branding Iron," telephone #258. There was a parking area at side where you parked your car, a fellow came out to take your order, took it inside where it was filled and would then deliver it to your car. The restaurant is currently occupied by Hunan Restaurant at 929 E. Elbert Street.

The Silver Grill restaurant was located on left of Hwy. 72E, almost at corner where you turned into Silk Mill. You could eat inside, or park in back, order, and they would deliver to car. It was located where parking area of Cobo's Used Cars is currently.

Chapter 15
Elberton's Barber Shops
Including Doug's Barber Shop

Remembrances from Ray Howell concerning the barber shops of Elberton in the early 50s.

Mr. Jim Maxwell and Mr. Tommy Howell had a shop in the basement of First National Bank (where Doug Anderson's shop is presently). When Mr. Maxwell retired Paul Webb bought the business and he, his dad and Tommy Howell ran the shop.

Later Mr. Howell opened a shop near his home in Rock Brach.

In the FNB shop there were facilities to take a shower and they supplied soap and towels at a cost of 25 cents. Ray tells that he used their facilities on Saturday Nights. They would still be open when he got off work from Winn-Dixie's meat department at 7 pm. Since he lived in Rock Branch, and his girlfriend Carolyn Dixon lived in Deep Creek, it would have been a total distance of 24 miles for him to travel so he would have been late for date time.

In 1944, Clyde Williams had a barber shop in the basement of Strand Theater. The theater burned and of all his equipment he only saved one chair. The Strand was located on West end of square where First Financial is now located.

Mr. Williams with Mr. Tiny Nash, then opened a shop on Oliver St. two doors above Cosby's poolroom. Martin Bagwell worked there shining shoes at 25 cents a shine. When he got another job Cecil Bond got his position. Later Wayne Brown worked there and saved enough money to purchase a black and white television for his parents.

Before Elbert St. was widened Mr. Tom McMullan had a barber shop between Williamson's grocery and Funny Powell's poolroom. That is where Doug Anderson began cutting hair.

On N. McIntosh St. Mr. Laurence McCall had a shop and Mr. Frank Slay worked for him. Mr. McCall later opened a shop near his home on Old Golf Course Rd. and Mr. Slay took over the shop. Mr. McCall ran his shop until his retirement in 2012 and Mr. Slay ran the N. McIntosh shop till shortly before his death in 2013.

Mr. Glenn Crider had a shop in a small building he built at the front of his home on Lower Heard St.

Mr. W. T. Varnum had a shop on N. McIntosh, about where Salvation Army is now located. His shop had a dirt floor and he practiced singeing your hair after cutting it. He took a piece of paper, set it afire, blew it out and used the hot edge to singe where he had cut. After cutting one customer and applying Vitalis Hair Tonic to his hair, he began singeing and the man's whole head caught fire. Needless to say it was quickly put out with damp shop towels. Joe Hall also used this practice of singeing but he used "a device similar to a sparkler." Doug Anderson says that he remembers a "tapering candle" being used for this procedure.

Mrs. Tom Carrington opened "Sportsmen's Barber Shop" under her office on Hartwell Hwy. and Tim Urtzberg and Alvis Florence worked there.

Hoke Tiller had a shop at his house on Lexington Hwy.

Mr. Willie Conwell had a shop in Bowman and the cost of a cut never changed, it was always 50 cents. At his death Bill Madden began cutting hair there.

Joe Hall opened a shop in the basement of his home and he also cut, washed and set women's hair.

For most of these, a haircut, shave with a straight razor and hot towels placed on face, the charge was $1.00.

From the Elberton Star -

"After being closed for several weeks while remodeling was being done, the Granite City Barber Shop, 158 McIntosh Street, is again open. A real up-to-date barber shop. Our motto is strictly sanitary and first-class service. No more old, filthy public drinking glass in our place. We furnish individual drinking cups to the public."

"You can get a shave at T. T. Coogler's barber shop at J. A. Maxwell's old stand for 15 cents, a haircut for 35 cents and have the work done by first class workingmen, too. The shop is sanitary and up to date in appointments. Two chairs.

Doug's Barber Shop

This shop, now owned by Doug Anderson, has been in business in downtown Elberton since 1919.

In 1956, Doug apprenticed with Mr. Tom McMullan when a haircut was 75 cents and a Coke was a nickel. At the time, Mr.

McMullan's shop was immediately behind the Pure gas station, which was on the corner of College Avenue and North Oliver Street.

Doug's shop is in the basement of the building originally built for First National Bank whose president was Mr. P. C. Maxwell. At construction time, Mr. Maxwell had a portion of the basement space set aside for a barbershop, which his brother Jim Maxwell ran. Paul Webb bought it in 1957 and in 1962, Doug Anderson and Bill Madden bought it. Bill stayed until 1968 and Doug has run it for more than 50 years.

The shop is filled with pictures galore of children men and boys whose hair Doug has cut. One picture is of a four-year-old who asked for a shave with his haircut, so Doug lathered him up and shaved him with the backside of his razor.

Many badges are on display from local Police, the State Patrol, EMT's and others, prompting the shop to be nicknamed the "Downtown Precinct."

There is a picture of David Hunt who was the first 18-year-old admitted to serve as an Elberton Police Officer. David later worked for the Georgia State Patrol and served as bodyguard for Georgia's Governor Roy Barnes.

Business cards of customers are stuck down one wall. Many key rings, all still intact, left in the shop over the years are laid out.

Two car tags, donated by A. B. Cleveland, 1961 and 1969 - both have tag numbers printed upside down.

There is a coffee set up and a Coke machine with a "Don't Go Round Hungry" sign attached.

A 1960 photo shows Billy Booth who was then the shoeshine boy having his hair cut by Doug, with Tom McMullan looking on. This was the final haircut of the 3000 hours Doug spent in the Apprentice Program to certify for the State Barber Board.

Boxes of toy Tanker Trucks, caps, hats, a Georgia flag, wooden JESUS signs, car tags along with combs, styptic pencils, suntan lotion, razor blades, and such, are for sale.

Hanging on the wall are two frames holding arrowheads that Doug has found and a large clock, fashioned by Jack Bell, Sr., with the numbers printed counter-clockwise, 11 is in place of 1, 10 in place of 2; it tells the correct time because the hands turn backward. The list could go on and on.

The shop address is 6 Oliver St. and is in the basement of, what is now, the Poole Building. The shop has three barber chairs and the one in the middle is original to the shop. When it stopped working Doug thought to purchase a new one but employee John Jenkins said, "No." They then took it apart, had the controls repaired, and it now works perfectly. There are also three wooden couches, a shoeshine rack and a hat rack, which are also original to the shop.

During the period from the 1920s through the 1940s, it was popular for men to take baths and showers at a barbershop since some homes did not have running water. Doug's shop had two tubs, and a coal fired heater to heat the water and was open 6 am until 11:00 pm Friday nights and 12:00 pm on Saturdays.

That Doug's Barbershop operates six days a week, when so many men now go to *women's* beauty salons for haircuts, speaks loudly to the value of personal attention and camaraderie in "the old time" tradition, while delivering up-to-date service.

Do You Remember When

Your family had a vegetable garden from which green beans, butter beans, corn, squash and okra where gathered? Then you had to help with shelling, stringing, shucking; then cooking over a hot stove, on a hot July/August day before placing them in canning jars. But, oh how good they were in the cold wintertime!

Chapter 16
Pitts Pool

Who remembers the Pitts Pool?

In 1940, this swimming pool was located between Dewy Rose and Bowman, on Brickyard Road, which is to the right of Highway 17. The pool was several hundred yards from where a brickyard was located in the early 1900s.

It is my understanding that at the time it was the only pool located in Elbert County. I've talked to several people who swam there. They had many good memories.

Concerning its size, it was a large pool, having shallow and deep ends. Several have likened it to the size of the Elberton City Pool that was built at a later date. It had a high dive "that some were foolish enough to dive off," according to one person.

It was filled by water from Beaverdam Creek and I was told it was c-o-l-d. The ditches dug to divert creek water into the pool were lined and there were several strainers to filter the water before it entered the pool. When the pool was full, the water was diverted back to the creek.

There were also bleachers for seating around the pool area. Mr. Dave Pitts owned the pool and Mr. Howard Brown, father of Florence B. Rowland and Allison Brown, had daily responsibility for its care.

Mr. Brown also ran a small "store" near the pool where he sold candy/cookies/drinks to pool patrons.

In the June 15, 2015 edition of the "Star" this was included in the "75 Years Ago" article: "Dave Pitts announces that he has just received a large shipment of new inner tube life-savers and bathing suits for the enjoyment of patrons of his swimming pool. He has a sufficient number to accommodate large picnic parties which are taking advantage of the rural beauty and delightful accommodations of his splendidly arranged pool"

Mrs. Rowland remember that in 1940, as her father was to be pool caretaker, her family moved into a large, four or five bedroom house which was near the pool.

Mr. Pitts, who was called "Uncle Dave" by everyone, lived in one bedroom of the house, but on weekends he moved to a room he kept at the Samuel Elbert Hotel in Elberton.

As the swimming cost was 25 cents per person, in the hot summer the pool was filled with "droves" of swimmers. It was the hang-out place for youth, especially on Saturday and Sunday.

One lady stated the fact that she met her future husband at the pool. When they were introduced she said, "Gosh, you are cute," and their relationship developed from there.

Another lady told me that it was 'the thing' for young people and that on various occasion her Sunday School class went there for picnics and swimming.

There was also a large well stocked fish pond behind the pool that was regularly used by local fishermen.

I've talked to the following people who swam there Lois Anderson, Ed Ayers, Sue (Fleming) Isom, Helen (Beasley) Ayers, Martha (Beasley) Fortson, Mildred Moss, Billy Neal, Florence (Brown) Rowland and Sallie (Lunsford) Seymour.

Did you ever swim there? What stories about your enjoyment of its facilities can you tell?

Chapter 17
The Elberton Brickyard

In February 1898, O. L. Stephenson leased 300 acres more or less from Mr. M. B. Adams with the right to build and operate a brickyard including the right to construct and operate a railroad and have full and free access to streams of water on the property. The lease was for 10 years at $100 per year. Mr. Wm. Ed (Gus) Wallis was superintendent when W. O. Jones purchased the brickyard from Mr. Stephenson and operated it as the Elberton Brick Company.

In December 1909, records show that Mr. Adams leased the property to the Elberton Brick Company with W. O. Jones, W. C. Wallis and A. F. Smith as principals. The lease was for eight years beginning January 1, 1910 and ending January 1, 1918 for payment of $950 with $200 upon signing, $300 on January 1, 1910 and $450 on February 1, 1910. This lease specifically included the right to use, appropriate and consume all the clay/dirt and convey and consume all the water from the streams on said land as needed for making bricks and such products.

Cabins were constructed near the plant for mostly black employees who worked from Monday morning until Saturday night, 10 hours a day. A mess hall was provided for meals. Mr. Wm. E.

Wallis, son of Gus Wallis, said, "Papa made certain that all workers got at least one good meal each day which included meat, cornbread and molasses. Peak production reached 50,000 bricks per day.

Men dug clay from pits and loaded onto carts. Trained mules hauled the carts to an incline where a cable arrangement pulled the carts to where clay was dumped into a mixing machine. A team of workers constantly fed the machines while others stacked the bricks as they came out. Bricks were then moved on carts down tracks to a drying station. After drying, the bricks were moved to one of five kilns where they were burned about four days.

The plant made several qualities of brick from the fine clay of the brickyard. The Southern Railroad had a sidetrack into the plant where finished bricks were loaded onto rail cars for shipment to buyers in many locations.

Several senior adults who were interviewed remembered the ponds created where clay was dug from the soil. Mark Neal tells of recent duck hunting in the brickyard area created by the ponds.

There was a smallpox epidemic at the brickyard just before it closed. One person who moved to the area in 1939 said he heard that officials wouldn't let people leave the brickyard when smallpox broke out. When so many died, they dumped the bodies into old wells and covered them with broken bricks. He said the plant had been abandoned many years but there were still ponds created in spots where clay had been dug. He was told by his father when hunting not to let his dogs dig in the ground of the brickyard because the smallpox germs might be dug up.

The brickyard also had a pottery business using the same clay used for the bricks. All types of jugs, pitchers and other items were fired there. It was located beyond the brickyard, on the right side of the road.

Katherine Fernandez has a "milk pitcher" which has a brown glaze with "Gunter" engraved on its bottom. It has always been in her family's home and although it has never been authenticated, she understands that it was made at the brickyard pottery.

It is said that the Brickyard ceased operations in 1918 because of shortages resulting from WWI when wood or coal, to fire the boilers could no longer be obtained.

*Do You
Remember When*

Good friends were hard to find, harder to leave, and impossible to forget!

Chapter 18
Jack and Jill Kindergarten

In 1947, Mrs. Katie Lou Brown opened Jack and Jill Kindergarten in Elberton Georgia. Before this time the small North Georgia town of Elberton had no kindergarten and as Mrs. Brown's youngest daughter was of age for this "pre-school" effort, she took on the project. Mrs. Brown had been a public school teacher but when she was expecting her first child, she had to leave that position—that was the requirement of the time. She now had a second child and had been at home with her two girls for about eight years and she wished to get back into the education process.

She publicized the fact that she would open the school and had many parents who wished their children to begin their education the year earlier than was offered in public schooling. Classroom availability was found at the local First (United) Methodist Church and Mrs. Brown began collecting suitable materials for the class. After it was collected, she decorated the room in Aa Bb Cc... posters, animal pictures, family pictures, appropriate seasonal decorations, etc.

I was five in July 1947, and we attended church with Mrs. Brown and her daughters Delaine 8, and Sherry 5, so we knew all the details and I was so thrilled when my parents enrolled me in the first class. My family did not have a car but Mrs. Sabra Thornton, mother of another enrollee Robert Thornton, picked up Maria Campos, Vernon Kidd, Audrey Jean Hill and myself and delivered us to the daily classes. I remember us standing (this was LONG before children's car-seats!) in the back and singing songs or reciting poems that we had previously learned in class.

Each day class began with prayer and the Pledge of Allegiance to the American Flag. We learned poems and songs and heard short stories as well as having almost daily craft activities. We learned a Bible verse for each letter of the alphabet—A, "A soft answer turneth away wrath"...

The church did not have a designated play area but Stilwell Elementary School, with its large playground, was only three short blocks away. On pretty days Mrs. Brown got out her 20 foot rope, designated a spot for each child on either side of the rope and with herself leading the way, we walked those three blocks. It was unheard of for a child to turn loose the rope, step into the street or onto one of the front lawns in the residential area through which we passed! If such an "accident" happened that child received a stern look from Mrs. Brown and "Now, Carolyn, you know better than that," which was all it took for that indiscretion to never happen again! After enjoying ourselves on the public school playground equipment, the kindergarteners returned to class in the same manner by which we had arrived.

At the end of the year we had graduation ceremonies where the girls wore long white dresses—mother made mine, of organdy–it was SO pretty - and the boys were in dark pants and a white shirt. For receipt of our diplomas each had a cap and gown and each moved the tassel from one side to the other on our mortar boards. An explanation of why this was done had to be explained, and we had to be shown how to achieve this important procedure.

Mrs. Brown taught kindergarten for 40+ years. She added a room that had two walls of floor to ceiling windows, to her home and after his retirement her husband, Mr. Easton, aided her. In fact, my three children were also her students—Mark in 1968, Melanie in 1970 and Mimi in 1972. For the last 20 years she had two classes, morning and afternoon.

Both her girls grew up, married and moved away and after Mr. Easton died you would see Mrs. Brown walking—to the post office, to the library, etc., until she was in her late 80's. She taught Sunday School to five and six-year-olds for 40+ years. The beloved Mrs. Brown died in October 2006 at the age of 98.

The Jack and Jill Kindergarten class picture was made on the side steps of the First (United) Methodist Church, Elberton, GA. Kindergarteners in cap and gown are:

1st row—Grady Thrasher, Audrey Jean Hill, Bobby Brown, Henry Wall, Mike Mewbourn, Roger Cosby

2nd row—Carl Brooks, Mary Minor Hawes, Annette Ward, Wayne Hunt, Sandra Gilbert, Billy Deadwyler

3rd row—Jimmy Yeary, Robert Thornton, Sherry L. Brown, Jeff Sanders

4th row—'Telle heard, Howell Teasley, Hugh Rambo, Roger Harris

5th row—Peggy Heard, Betty Vanover, Carolyn Johnson, Marcia Oglesby

6th row—Maria Campos, Barbara Albertson, Sandra Manahan, Dale Williamson, Rita Lee

7th row—Vernon Kidd, Billy Fortson, John Comolli,

Undergraduates shown, not in cap and gown were Phil Butler and Brenda Walton

Chapter 19
The Burning of Central School

On Monday November 7, 1955 Central School Burned.

The building had been constructed in 1909 and opened for classes in early February 1910. The cause of the fire was never declared that I know of, but I think that the fact that as all classroom and hallway floors were wood which had been infused with oil, was a big "help" to the fire. This has been corroborated by two people with whom I've talked. (Harold Jones and Carolyn Miller).

Originally it was a school for all eleven, then twelve, grades. As the town's population of children increased that building was no longer able to hold all 12 grades, but I'm not sure what year that change was made. The School Board dictated that further sixth graders would go to Stillwell Elementary and seventh went to Stevens Elementary.

When Central burned I had just begun 8th grade which meant I was in "high" school - as there was no middle school in 1955. On the day of burning the fire was so large that fire men and trucks from Hartwell, Athens and Anderson aided in containing the fire to the classroom area of the school. Grades 1-5 classes were still held in the building.

Carolyn Miller told me that she had girls' basketball practice in the rock gym that afternoon and when she left about 5:00 p.m., she took Ann Williams (Gunter) home as Ann lived about a quarter mile before her home. When she got to her home, her mother told her the school was burning. She immediately returned to the school and she and Coach Lee Atkinson began gathering all the sports equipment/uniforms that were in the rock gym into one room, "which was similar to a vault" was her quote. After that they went up to the actual school area and helped remove equipment from the building.

Linda B. Avery told that Eleanor Spalding called her about the burning and when she and her family went out front of their house on Athens Hwy., they could see the red glow. She and her family then got in their car and went to see the actual burning. Cecil bond says he sat on the grass in front of "the Colley house" (Magnolia Estates) and watched the burn. People from all over town came to watch.

All materials–teacher's documents, memoranda, maps, blackboards, chalk and erasers were gone. The case of trophies that former sports teams had garnered were burned. Since the fire occurred after school hours, there was no one inside and kids were home and most had their textbooks with them. Because the Commercial class was in the basement, some typewriters were saved by individuals who came to the scene and hand-passed them one to another to the outside. I've been told a piano was also removed.

The night of the fire I understand that Mr. Cecil Palmer, who taught Shop at the time, stood outside his class building and climbed onto its roof with a water hose and thoroughly wet that wooden structure so that it did not burn. In that building, Shop class was on the first floor and entered from the front. Mr. F. M. Young held Agriculture classes in the basement which had a back entrance. There was an elongated wooden building beside the shop that had three or four classrooms in it. I don't know if Mr. Palmer also kept it wet, but neither did that building burn. These two buildings were located about where the drive is beside the "Inferno" (the current basketball gym). Classes held in this elongated building were Civics and Remedial Math taught by Carolyn Miller, Social Studies by Coach McMillan and DCT taught by Mr. Robert Deane.

The next morning a blaze erupted and the auditorium that was attached to the backside of the school burned. For several days the local National Guard was called out to police the area and keep persons from attempting to go into the burned area.

Oh, the questions that were asked - Are we going to be out of school for the rest of the year? We're not going to have to go to Hartwell for school are we? There was no facility in Elberton large enough to hold all the kids and no place with a lunchroom. And you can't go to school without lunch we thought. The Holy Trinity Lutheran Church was the first to offer use of its facility. The school board and city officials decided to request use of the facilities at the First Methodist and First Baptist Churches which were only a block apart. When asked, both churches agreed.

From First Baptist Minutes: "In November of 1955, while the town slept, a fire quickly spread and completely destroyed the Elbert County High School building. A call meeting of the deacons provided relief, as the educational facilities (Of the church) were made available to the Board of Education for emergency use. The joint facilities of nearby First Methodist Church provided temporary classrooms until a new building could be constructed to replace the burned building. Painting and minor repairs were made after two and one-half years use."

Classes began only a week after the burning with classes starting at 8:00 a.m. each day, ending at 1:15, there was no lunchroom, so we went home for lunch. English, History and language classes were held in the First Baptist Sunday School area. Math and science classes were held in the Sunday School area of First Methodist, with Home Economics in the house immediately behind the FMC sanctuary. The typing class was held in the basement-like room at the rear of the Methodist sanctuary building. Band practice was held in a large room in the Harris-Allen Library which was next door to First Methodist.

After classes began in the churches a school bus would park in what is now the corner parking area, Thomas and Church Street of The Rock of FBC. Students would load to be carried to shop, Ag and DCT in their respective classrooms at the former school which had not burned. The PE classes were held in the Rock Gym. Mr. Cecil Palmer drove the bus back and forth to classes. There was a 10 minute break between classes which benefited those who had to change churches for their next class. I remember getting wet from rain when I walked from church to church. Cecil Palmer also always drove the bus called "The Blue Goose" that carried the Elberton ball-players to all out-of-town games.

Before the fire, grades 1-5 and 8-12 were held in the Central School building. After the burn I don't know how 1st - 7th elementary classes were divided between Stilwell and Stevens schools.

When you walked up the front steps of Central, the school office was on the immediate right. Down the right hallway, on the right, was the office of Principal, Mr. J. D. Messer.

On the left of that hallway, across from the principal's office was Miss Goodwin's Biology and a math classes.

Grades 1-4 were in the hallway straight in the front as you came in the front door. Just beyond those classes were steps down to the basement hall which led to the auditorium, rest rooms, lunch room or outside if you were going to recess.

On the left of the entrance was the school nurse's office, Mrs. Parsons. Fifth grade, taught by Miss Maude Eavenson, was the first door on the right down the left hallway and Miss Margaret Martin's high school English class was the first door on the left of that hallway. Home Economics classes, taught by Martha Britt (Jones) had their kitchen on the left and sewing room on the right in that hallway.

The basement front rooms, held the lunchroom, with Mrs. Nathleen Cleveland, Director. Commercial classes (typing and shorthand) with Miss Parrish and Miss Robertson, were taught across the hall from the lunchroom. Chemistry class, taught by Mrs. Margaret Bryan, was held on the Forest Avenue front side with the Chemistry lab on the back side. Linda Bishop Avery said they had been doing experiments concerning oxygen and some of the "boys" said they caused the fire. The two restrooms, Girls, overseen by Carol Cook and Boys, overseen by Cliff Downer, were in the middle with entrances and exits beside the lunchroom and the auditorium.

On the second floor the library, librarian Mrs. N. R. Haworth; covered the area where grades 1-4 were downstairs. Classes for Latin, Mrs. Janie Dell Gaines; Spanish and English. Mrs. Laodice Burt; Geometry, Mrs. L. W. New; Algebra, Mrs. Mozelle Teasley; English taught by Esther Johnson were all on the second floor.

Other teachers were: Coach Bob Armstrong, Science and Math; "Chunk" Atkinson, P.E. and football: R. G. Bryan, Math; Betty Goodman, Science and Guidance Counselor; James Knight, English; Evelyn Leroy, Chorus; George MacMillan, Social Studies and Boys Basketball; Arnoldina Thornton, History; Carolyn Miller, Civics and Girls Basketball.

The Band, whose director was Mary Jo Andrews, met upstairs in the auditorium and when the burn began, individuals went upstairs to throw the instruments, in their cases, out the windows. Linda Bishop Avery told me that after being thrown out a window her trumpet played fine but her case was never the same.

Graduation - In 1956 they had the Baccalaureate Service in the First Baptist Sanctuary and the graduation service was to be held in the Granite Bowl for the first time. Carolyn Miller told me she helped to set up the folding chairs for the graduates. But in the afternoon of graduation there came a terrible rain storm with a strong wind that blew some chairs for the graduates flat, so the service was held in the Rock Gym; it was blistering hot in there. Linda B. Avery remembers her family sitting on the pull-out seats used for basketball games. She said the graduates were told if they did not get the certificate with their name on it, just to take it, move their tassel and exit the Stage. They would clear up any discrepancies the *next* week.

The school did not have a fight song to be played or sung at football games so, to make one available, Jackie (Wall) Coogler, who graduated in 1947, wrote lyrics and collaborated with Mr. R. Glen Johnson,, the band director during the 1940s - 1950s, who wrote the music. Do you remember the words?

"Oh, we love our dear old school
And the devils blue and white.
They can give it and can take it,
For the things they think are right.

It will be our fame and glory.
And for EHS we'll win
For our dear old school and colors
We will fight and not give in.

Faithful and loving, forever we will be
For our school and alma mater
Hats off for the blue and white!"

Thanks to Marvin Hardy, Jr. for the completion of lyrics I did not know.

Classes were held in the churches for three years. We went back to the new school, which is now city and county government offices, when I was in the eleventh grade, in September 1958.

Do you Remember Stony Williams? He was the living "mascot" for the Blue Devils.

When Elberton would play Hartwell basketball, he would get so mad when he went into the Hartwell gym. Possibly because he was hassled by Hart participants. (Rita L. Thompson) One year he was given a football jacket which he wore everywhere. Do you remember the year?

Another 8th grader, Peggy H. Galis, remembers that three of her jackets burned because at different times she had left them at the school.

Do you remember Mr. Messer installing the system of giving demerits for any bad classroom conduct or school grounds misdemeanors?

Sandra McLanahan Worley told me that after the remains of the burned building were cleared she and friends went there and skated on the concrete basement flooring that remained. Sarah Lesseur reported the same.

Peggy (Heard) Galis tells that in Mrs. Janie Dell Gaines class for school, which just happened to be her normal Sunday School classroom, Mrs. Gaines would begin each class with prayer, "God continue to bless my good students and please help Roger Cosby, and Peggy Heard."

Rita L. Thompson remembers that during assemblies of all classes, Superintendent Mr. Haworth would leave an item envelope in a seat and if a student picked it up, opened and read, they would receive a prize–such as lunch with Mr. Haworth. Who were the prize winners?

Chapter 20
Snuggling Birds

Look, look - those little birds are snuggling together. Aren't they cute? Wonder why they landed on my deck? I have seed feeders out and there are always all types of birds flying in to feed. Wonder if these will eat the seed types that are in the feeders? Maybe some bread scraps, or fruit. I've got some apples and bananas they might eat. Or maybe I'll make a suet cake for them to enjoy.

Some birds, like the Black Capped Chickadee, flies to the feeder, picks a single seed in its beak, then flies to a nearby tree to peck at that seed against the limb on which he lands. And he doesn't fly in a straight line he flies in a rising/sinking wavily motion The Tufted Titmouse will immediately eat whatever type of seed he gathers from the feeder. And Cardinals, because they are a larger bird, sometime act like they own the feeder. When they fly in many smaller birds fly away as the Cardinals stay and eat all they want. And the Sparrows come regularly. The Wren, with their tails straight up in the air, are also frequent visitors. Many times they have made a nest inside the narrow opening left at the top of one of the iron poles that support the back of the deck. I have watched them enter, and exit the pole, but can't figure out how they get in that small opening!

When I put out meal worms, I use them dried, not the wiggly/crawly live ones, Blue Birds come to feed. One year Blue Birds even made a nest in a birdhouse nailed to the outside of a wooden deck post.

The Robins, Blue Jays and Mockingbirds will not eat from the feeders. Sometimes they will hop around on the ground below the feeders and feast off the seeds dropped on the ground. Doves do this on a regular basis.

Maybe these snuggling birds are sparrows. They look like they are pleased with themselves so maybe their last baby has fledged and they have no more responsibility for their little ones. Now they can find an area where ground has been plowed so they can easily find worms, or a nearby birdbath where they can splash in the water. Or they might just use the time to fly around, checking out the scenery, which they've not been able to do while they had a full nest to keep fed. But, as they look so satisfied, maybe they've just gone back to their empty nest to snuggle together! I'm just going to leave them alone and let them enjoy their happy time.

Chapter 21
Nancy and I

I was born on 7 July, 1942, eight forty-five am, at Thompson-Johnson Hospital in Elberton GA. At ten pm the same day another baby girl was born at Thompson-Johnson. Our mothers knew each other, but were not close friends. We don't know why but I was named Martha Carolyn and she was named Nancy Carolyn. My family called me Carolyn and her family called her Nancy.

She had a brother who was six years older. So did I. She had a sister three years older and I have a sister three years younger.

We grew up in a small north Georgia town. She lived in a new sub-division home her family purchased near the town lake. I grew up moving from rental to rental until the 1950 rental of an older two story home, where my family then lived for 16 years. We lived on a busy street only three blocks from the town square.

Nancy and I began first grade at Central School which had been built in 1909 to house all eleven, grades of public school.

Later, of course, the twelfth grade was incorporated into the space. She and I had not been around each other during our first five years, but we were now in first grade together and became good friends. We continued classes through fifth grade, always having the same teachers. We had sleepovers and I remember thinking how nice and small her home was.

As I've said mine was a big, old two story and my brother had one and my sister and I had the other of the upstairs bedrooms. The front two rooms and bath upstairs, were a small apartment where an elderly, (I thought at the time), unmarried lady was tenant. She also used the hall for her icebox and desk. She was very friendly and I'm sure now it was a trying time for her to have 5, 8, 14 year olds sleeping, and playing, so close to her bedroom!

By the year Nancy and I were in fifth grade the town population had grown and there was no longer room at Central for students of twelve grades. The decision was made to send all sixth graders to Stilwell and all seventh graders to Stevens thereby leaving space at Central for all high school grades. These were the two elementary schools which our town had built many years before. Both of us had begun classes at Central because we lived in its area. But she now went to Stilwell and I went to Stevens.

When we reached eighth grade in 1955, we went back to Central for high school. It sure was a contrast from elementary school for we now had a homeroom teacher and then had to travel to different rooms with different teachers for the five classes we took!

We didn't truly get accustomed to high school before Central school building burned in November of that year.

The school burned so we won't have to go to school anymore was the exclamation of many students. But we were out only one week as the school board had made plans of new locations for us to continue classes.

The First Baptist and First Methodist churches were only a block apart and after their individual church conferences, both had decided that their Sunday School areas could be used for public school. We would still change classes but sometime we had to walk between the two churches for assigned classes. The time between classes was extended to ten minutes giving time to walk that extra distance. All English, history, language classes were taught at First Baptist. All math, science and Home Ec were taught at First Methodist. The band met for practice in the Masonic Hall that was next to First Methodist. A school bus was run to the Central grounds where phys ed was taught in the Rock Gym and Shop and Agriculture were taught in a separate wooden building that did not burn.

That they did not burn is a story in itself for there were two wooden buildings on the Central campus that did not burn. Mr. Cecil Palmer, who taught Shop in one of the buildings, at different times climbed atop both buildings with a water hose to wet them down to keep sparks from setting them on fire. It was a heroic feat he accomplished!

School classes in the churches were from eight am to one pm when school was let out for kids to go home for lunch. I never thought about it at the time but I'm sure that caused many problems for families who were accustomed to having lunch provided for their kids at school.

Nancy and I continued to be friends through the years. In fact a new modern school was being built on the same property Central had stood. Where Central had been three stories with grounds, huge oak trees and a play area, the new one was only for high school students and was one story spread out over the complete lot.

We began classes at the new school in September, 1958 when she and I were in the eleventh grade and we had some of the same classes. I remember Miss Britt teaching us Home Ec, Miss Hardie and Miss Parrish teaching us typing and shorthand, and Miss Arnoldina Thornton *trying* to teach us all those history dates. Both of us even took Latin from Mrs. Janie Dell Gaines.

About the time we got in the new school we were sixteen, and *boys* came to our attention! The TAHO Club, Teen Age Hang Out, had been built on a portion of the school property. It was great to meet all our friends there on Friday and Saturday nights to dance, eat chips and drink Coke. There was no smoking inside and at the time smoking was not a big problem.

It also seemed that Nancy and I had the same tastes in boyfriends. We each dated others but there were two that we each particularly liked. She would "go steady" with one and I would "go steady" with the other. We'd break up and after a while we would switch the ones with whom we went steady. This went on for a couple of years, but she and I were good friends and never got irritated with one another.

Both boys had cars, one was a '59 Ford and the other a '57 Chevy. I don't remember exactly how it was planned, but the four of us decided to double date one night! We went to the local drive-in for a double-feature! After watching the first movie the boys went to the concession stand for pop-corn and coke. Following our plans while the boys were gone, Nancy and I changed seats! So, we spent the first movie with one boy and the second movie with the other boy! This happened in the fall of 1959.

Nancy married at age eighteen, and I married at age twenty, but not to either of those boys who had been our steadys.

Nancy and her husband had a son, who is a pastor, and a daughter who teaches school. Her husband died after fifty-three years of marriage.

I have been married fifty six+ years and have a son who is an engineer and two daughters who are in marketing/sales.

Nancy and I now live 35 miles apart but we, with some other school friends, meet once a month for lunch and chit-chat. That's what long-time friends are for.

Chapter 22
Birds and Snakes

I love to sit outside in the Spring sunshine. How can anyone not believe in God when they see new leaves budding out on 'dead' trees, green grass coming up where all the lawns had been brown, feeling the warmth of His sun outside when in January you had been out in that same sun and it didn't even feel warm?

I had cooked homemade soup that morning. Cecil and I had each eaten a full bowl with crackers for lunch and I planned to divide what was left and take it to some widow friends. Anybody can open a can I thought, but it's better when you've made a large container mixing corn, okra, several kinds of beans, tomatoes and beef bouillon for flavor. And my friends had stated many times how difficult it was to cook for just one.

While it was cooling I decided to sit outside in the beautiful sunshine and read more from my library book. The sun was bright and there was a small breeze so I pulled my chair to the edge of the carport and sat down expecting an enjoyable hour.

What now served as carport had originally been a patio when our kids were still at home. It is at the rear of the house, still open ended but now covered by the deck Cecil had added several years ago. I settled in a lounge chair and opened my book.

Only after reading a couple of paragraphs I began hearing a bird making chp, chp sounds. They were not like the usual bird cheep, cheep's, but sounded as if the bird was in distress. As I looked up I saw not one, but two birds, flying and lighting, flying and lighting, at different places all around the yard. I watched for a minute but could make nothing of their flights so I went back to my book.

The car was parked not ten feet in front of my chair and suddenly one of the birds landed on the car hood, looked straight at me, and continued the chp, chp distress sounds. As that was as close as any bird had ever landed near me I knew something had to be wrong. As I stood from my chair, the bird flew and as I took one step toward the rear of the car I saw - a snake!!

It was now crawling on the concrete of the patio. Somehow it had slithered up the brick wall, out over the rafters and knocked down the nest and three baby birds. I had previously noted that a bird had placed a nest on one of the I-beams on which the deck was constructed for it was immediately above where we opened the trunk of our SUV. I didn't have a clue how the snake could have knocked that bird nest down. Could he have slithered up the brick wall of the house and out the I-beam to reach the nest? How would he have known the nest was there? Why did I not see that snake when I came out, I wondered? I might have been able to, somehow, keep it away from that nest. Now what?

I immediately yelled for my husband and when he stuck his head out the door I told him there was a snake and asked him to come *do something* about it. He brought his gun, thinking he would shoot it but the snake was slithering across the concrete so he could not shoot onto that surface. He walked around to the rear of the car and yelled "Here's another one". He shot at the second snake but it went into the thick Monkey Grass that was planted beside the drive.

When he turned back to the first snake he saw it crawling up one of the back tires of the car!! He bammed on the car tail pipe with the stock of his gun. No results. He got in and cranked the car and revved it. Still no results. So, he put the car in gear and drove out the drive and down the highway - exceeding the speed limit, I am sure! He kept watch in the rearview mirror and when he saw the snake fall out, he quickly turned the car around and drove over the snake thereby killing it.

When Cecil returned he again looked for the second snake but could not find it. The tiny baby birds did not survive the ten foot fall onto concrete, so I had disposed of them.

With all that drama I had lost interest in my book so I went back inside, divided the soup and delivered it to three friends.

After our evening meal I again went outside to read and of course had to look where the second snake had been - and there he was! Again, I yelled for Cecil who, this time, got a hoe as his weapon and as he got near the snake, chopped *off* its head.

Using the hoe, he picked up the dead snake and took it to the edge of a nearby wooded area and hung it in a tree. Hanging a dead snake in a tree has given rise to the belief that it would be a sign for rain, and rain was always welcome in this farming area.

We both know snakes are part of God's creatures, but both of us are very 'apprehensive' of snakes and our worldly thoughts are that the only good snake is a dead one!

That is an experience I won't forget but I hope never to have that happen again!

The above happened in the Spring of 2017. In Spring 2018 the same bird, I assume, built a nest in the exact spot that was used in 2017. It has done the same in 2019. I believe the bird is a Junco for it has a gray back and a white underside. For the past two years she has hatched three babies that have fledged and flown away.

Chapter 23
Johnson Life

My paternal grandparents were James William Johnson and Verona Payne Maxwell. Both were born in the Deep Creek and Fork Creek Baptist Church areas of northeast Elbert County GA.

After marriage they lived in that same area and sharecropped. Several years later they moved near Iva SC, again sharecropping. Then they moved to Biltmore, NC, and he worked in a "bleachery." I don't understand exactly what type of mill that was. They then moved to the Palmetto Community of Oglethorpe County, Georgia, again sharecropping.

Over the years they had seven children of which my daddy, F. A. born in 1909, was the oldest. My granddaddy Johnson died from pneumonia in January, 1930, leaving my grandmother with children aged: Daddy, 21; Bill, 20; Elizabeth, 17; Imogene, 15; Pete, 12; Julia, 7; and Frances, 4. My grandmother and the older boys still sharecropped. All the younger ones remember picking cotton, peas, etc., and also having a big family garden from which they canned anything that was not eaten when fresh picked. This was in the 1930's - there was no Social Security to aid my grandmother. How did she make it?

My grandmother's name was Verona. All the neighbors called her "Miss Rona" but the first grandchild could only say Nona, so that is what all thirteen of the grandchildren called her. In 1938, when Nona's youngest was 12, her second daughter, age 22, who was married, died of pneumonia leaving a five-year-old daughter which my grandmother took to raise.

I never knew Nona when she lived alone with her children. By the time I was born, 1942, she was living with one of her daughters and her husband. He worked at the Silk Mill in nearby Elberton and they lived in the village surrounding the mill. Later they moved back to Palmetto and lived in a four room house he had rented. My family lived in Elberton and it was always called 'going to the country' when we traveled there for a visit. And to me, we were always going to Nona's - it never entered my mind that she lived with her daughter and son-in-law, rather than them, and their son, living with her!

Their house was heated by a fireplace in the living room and a wood cook stove in the kitchen. Beside the kitchen stove a door opened into a small pantry. It had shelves that were lined with jars filled with the result of their summer canning. The large tin tub used for bathing, the tin dishpan and large crocks of meal and flour, along with the cleaned slop jar were also stored there. I remember white washing the stone front of the fireplace. Boy was that a treat! I remember sleeping with Nona on a cold winter night. Her bed had flannel sheets but, as usual, I pulled my legs up in a ball to get warm. She told me if I would stretch out my legs would then be near hers and they would get warm. It worked! That slop jar was under the edge of the bed for use at night. Daytime you always went to the outhouse behind her back yard.

Her bedroom was the walk-though room between the living room and kitchen. It had no closet and she had hung an extra flannel sheet across a corner, hung her few clothes behind it thereby making a closet.

The well with its angled tin roof was in the middle of the back yard. It was another treat to be allowed to let the metal bucket down into the water, then turn the heavy metal handle to pull the full bucket to the top. But, it was not always full when it got to the top! The back porch had a shelf which extended along its the entire outer edge and on this shelf was an enameled bucket of well water. Beside it was a metal dipper that was used by everyone who wanted a drink of that cool water *(Germs were unknown in that day)*. Also on that shelf was another enamel pan, round and about five inches deep, with a bar of soap nearby. You dipped your dirty hands into the water and used the soap to wash them. A piece of toweling hung on a nearby nail which you used to dry your hands.

The front yard was of white sand and it had to be swept as the last chore before bedtime. If you saw a blade of grass you had to pull it up!

In front of the house was a dirt road with a gulley on each side. On the house side of the road there was a wooden plank across the gulley to enable you to step into the yard without falling, or getting your feet wet if water was standing in that gulley. There was a double seat swing on the front porch and I remember swinging away many an afternoon singing *She'll be coming around the mountain...*.

In the back yard there was a smoke house with hams and sausage hanging to cure. These were the result of their "hog killing day" in November. For the kitchen stove and the fireplace there was a large pile of wooden puncheons and small slabs my uncle had gotten from a nearby sawmill. In the summer we used to pull the bark loose from a rounded piece of the puncheon and use corn silks to make a bed for our dolls. And there were always friendly hunting dogs in the yard.

Washday called for the following: building a fire, always in the same spot; heating water in a black iron washpot, adding soap flakes, stirring until the flakes "melted" then placing the clothes to be washed inside the pot. You had to punch the clothes down with a wooden paddle, which was ONLY used in this effort, then pulling out what had to be scrubbed on a rubboard. How did Nona's hands stand that HOT water? They were then wrung out, placed in a large tin tub (used for baths at other times) of rinse water, wrung out again then hung on the clothesline or the chicken wire fence that bounded the side yard. The clothesline was of metal wire strung between the smokehouse and a pole embedded in the yard.

About 100 yards above the house, on the other side of that dirt road, was the Palmetto Christian Church. They had Sunday School every week, but only had preaching once a month. The church was never locked and after I began piano lessons, with Nona's permission, I would go up to the church to *practice.* I did not have my practice music so I used the church hymnbook.

On the same side of the road as Nona's house, but about 60 yards away, with a cotton field between, lived Aunt Bart and Uncle Pat. Barto was Nona's sister and John Wiley Patton was the name of her husband. Their rented house had three rooms - kitchen, living room which also had their bed in it and a bedroom used for company. They had no children and helped Nona as she raised hers without a husband. Sometimes my family would spend the night at their home. Aunt Bart made the best biscuits and chocolate pies. She would take a cold biscuit, stick her finger in its side, fill it with her homemade muscadine jelly and boy was it good. Or in the summer she would split one open, place a slice of tomato inside, cover it with sugar and that was another delight! And those chocolate pies cooked in her wood stove were so-o-o good! She had a tall cabinet with tin doors at the top, pierced as a pie safe, and wooden doors at the bottom. In the middle it had a shelf, similar to a Hoosier cabinet. That cabinet shelf was her only space to mix, make biscuits, etc. There was a homemade wooden table in the kitchen and its only seating were wooden benches on either side.

Their house was not walled on the inside, the joists were sticking out, and they had placed large sheets of cardboard between the joists to aid in keeping out the cold. Once my younger sister and I were left with them for a short while and, as they had no paper, they allowed us to write on the cardboard. Boy was that a mistake!

When daddy and mama got back and saw what we had done we couldn't sit down for a while! All the time we were getting a spanking Aunt Bart was fussing at my daddy, "I told them they could," she would say. But we should have, and in reality we did, know better!

I mentioned their "guest" bedroom. One winter night daddy and mother, my sister and I spent the night there. The room had two double beds in it, both with high oak headboards and rounded footboards. When Eloise and I were put to bed Aunt Bart brought a straight chair and placed beside our bed *to keep us from falling out*. A few minutes after mother and daddy got in their bed in came Aunt Bart with a piece of toweling she had heated over their coal stove and wrapped it around my daddy's bald head *so it wouldn't get cold*. He accepted it but when she left he had a few 'choice' words to say as he removed it!

Uncle Pat use to walk us to the country store just down the road to buy us a Nehi chocolate milk. He always walked with a cane that could open to a seat for him to use if needed.

This was an idyllic childhood. None of the families had excess money but they all had enough to purchase any need. Sometime there was even enough to purchase a 'want.' And if there was a special need the families joined together to help. As when the granddaughter Nona raised wished to become a Registered Nurse, several of the uncles joined in to pay for her schooling to accomplish her wish.

In the cemetery behind that Christian Church lie the bodies of Nona and Grandpa Johnson (whom I never knew) and Uncle Pat and Aunt Bart. Several of us grandchildren visit there with flowers at least twice a year.

Chapter 24
Cleveland Family Furniture

My grandparents, Edwin Fortson and Mary Ella (Vickery) Cleveland were married on 28 November 1909. He was born 11 October 1868, and she was born 1 January 1872 which made him 41, and her 37 years old when they married and neither had previously been married. She was the fifth of the thirteen children of Reverend William James and Lettie Evelyn (Haynes) Vickery; and he was the fifth of the five children of Reuben Weston and Mary Victoria (Fortson) Cleveland.

To say they were "poor as church mice" is not a fabrication, concerning their young family.

I don't know the exact facts about the places they moved, but I know they never lived in the same place for any extended length of time. At various times he worked at the Elbert County water station, farmed with his father in the Centerville Community, worked for the state as an overseer for the building of the second Highway 72 bridge across Broad River, and at another time lived in Madison County, GA.

Because they did not have finances to purchase all the furniture in their houses, they had some of it handmade. I know this because my mother, their daughter, Lucile, inherited three of those pieces one of which is a kitchen table. The table top which is five feet by three feet is made from Poplar wood, but it's not one wide sheet of wood, it is made of three pieces: two are 15 inches wide and the third is 8 inches wide. The corners are rounded and its legs and under framing are made of pine and the Poplar boards are nailed to this frame with ten penny nails! And in the nailing they left 1/4 inch spaces between each board. At the ends of each 15 inches board there are splits in the wood about 6 or 7 inches long. All the years my Johnson family used the table it was covered in oil cloth and as each piece of oil cloth became worn it was covered with another piece of a different design.

My family never had any other kitchen table. We ate seated around it all the years I remember beginning in 1949 to 1963 when I left home. My parents continued using it until 1970 when they moved to a smaller house and the table was passed on to me and my new family.

My husband and I wanted to re-do the table and we began by removing the pieces of oil cloth. They had been tacked to the underside, and it was easy to pull out the tacks and remove the oil cloth - except on the rounded corners where it had become almost imbedded in the wood. When we finally dislodged it we found the corners had been rounded by a knife for they had short cuts, they were not smooth as they had felt under the oil cloth. When we stripped the top, we found that the Poplar wood had green colored stretches in each plank. After stripping, we sanded it and put five coats of polyurethane, with light sanding after each of the first four coats. It now looks beautiful, very rustic, but suits my style exactly.

The second piece was originally used as a meal bin. This was of prime use in former kitchens to hold the meal and flour that was regularly utilized in the making of bread. Its dimensions are 36 inches long, 13 inches wide and 24 inches high. Inside it is divided into two bins each $15^{1/2}$ by $15^{1/2}$ by $12^{1/2}$ Inches. The inside wood was sawed or sanded smooth. The front, back and top boarding are of unfinished pine. The two ends and bottom piece are also of pine, but have been smoothed. It is also put together with ten-penny nails.

I have written records that the kitchen table and the meal bin were constructed by Mr. Denver Harvell. Both these pieces were in our home for all my growing-up years.

The third piece I use as an end table. It is 29 inches high and has two 12 inch boards across the top that are 28 inches long and are again nailed with ten-penny nails. It has a drawer that is five inches deep and has a large, what looks like a wooden spool, serving as the drawer pull. Its four legs are beveled from two inches at bottom. It was never smoothed by a sander, but over the years the pine wood still has ridges in it which have become almost smooth. If the sunlight ever directly hits it, you can see remnants of blue paint. I've been told that this was buttermilk paint. The outer edges of the top show that they have been sawn. The family story that has been told is that the table top extended six to eight inches on either side and that once when the Cleveland family moved it was too wide for where my grandmother wanted it placed and my grandfather sawed off the side extensions making it fit where needed.

My grandparents had four children, Mary Lettie, DOB 18 August 1910; Willie Lucile, DOB 18 February 1912; James Weston, DOB 14 March 1913; and Adele who died at birth about a year later. From these known dates I have figured that they had four children by their sixth wedding anniversary. My grandmother had a severe case of arthritis and I've been told she was not able to stand holding her third child after sitting to nurse him. My grandfather died in 1953 at age eighty five and my grandmother in 1963 at age ninety one.

Chapter 25
Birds Flying South

I'm a Georgia great grandma and I've lived in this town my whole life, and most of the time that's fine by me. But in the late fall when the sky fills with birds migrating south for the winter, traveling thousands of miles, I get homesick for the places I've never been. Places like - Brazil, a huge country in South America.

Since I can't go, I'm going to pretend I'm a migrating Robin and see if she might travel to my favorite place.

They tell me that the egg I was in, that my mother laid, was a beautiful blue color. I was only a tiny fuzz ball the first few days of my life, but my mother kept finding worms and small bugs to feed me until I grew enough to fly by myself. Now I have a grayish-brown back and wings, but my belly is a beautiful orange. And I also have a yellow bill that has a black tip on it. That black tip helps me when I am pulling a luscious worm out of the ground for my supper. They say I'm very industrious and very authoritarian. I don't understand that last part about being authoritarian. I know I don't let other birds tell me what to do or run me off from just plowed ground where there are good worms, but that's just looking out for myself. It's not being authoritarian.

I had been in Georgia all summer. The lady of the house must have known who I was for she had been feeding me by throwing out delicious bread scraps for food. Many times she spread it out near the chair where she sat. As she sat there regularly, I got use to her being there and one day when I was eating and had my back turned to her she reached down and grabbed me. It wasn't a forceful grab; she held me very easy. But while she held me in her hand, the man who lived in that house attached a very small plastic wire to one of my legs. It sure scared me. Since it was almost time to migrate south when she turned me loose I decided to leave with the first group of migrating Robins.

We flew south, south, south. We even flew over a lot of water when there wasn't a place to land. As soon as we did reach land I stopped flying and landed on the sand. I was very thirsty and since there was a lot of water close by I took a drink. It was salty! Don't they know that salty water just makes you thirstier? There were a lot of bushes beside the sand and since bushes need water—but not salty water—to grow, I flew into them and found a small stream of good fresh water.

I continued flying south until I reached a HUGE statue of a man and I landed on the tip of one of his fingers. Both his arms were stretched out to the side and it looked like he wanted to give me a great big hug. Since I was hungry, I flew down to the ground and pulled up a worm. I tasted it but it tasted funny. Had someone spilled chili powder where the worm had been eating?

I flew up to a small tree that was near a park bench where two women were sitting. As I listened, they talked as funny as the worm had tasted. Then another woman came up, asked a question that I could understand, and the two women told that they had been speaking in Portuguese. No wonder I couldn't understand them.

I flew around the next day and saw a sign that said the HUGE man I landed on at first was the statue named "Christ the Redeemer" and that he was 98 feet tall. I could read the sign because it was written in English. It also said he was one of the 7 wonders of the new world. Wonder what was the old world? It all seems the same to me. And that statue is located in a city called Rio de Janeiro which is in Brazil, which is in South America. I had never flown that far south before.

As I flew around I saw another bird that had landed near a river. Its feathers were a beautiful yellow, and red, and orange. I later learned that it was, I have a hard time pronouncing it, a Toco Toucan. Reckon it has any relation to the taco locos that people eat at Mexican restaurants up in Georgia? I have heard that they taste spicy. I kept following the path of that river, but I finally quit flying and landed in what looked like a playground area. When I landed two children were sitting nearby and they read out of their history book that that river, the Parana, was the second longest in the world. It was 3,030 miles long. I sure was smart to land for I would have been exhausted if I had ever made it to its source.

As I stopped flying to again eat more of their chili tasting worms, I realized that the wire that had been tied to my leg had come loose. I shook and shook my leg till it finally fell off. One of the kids nearby had been watching me and he came over to pick up what I had shaken off. I flew into a nearby tree and watched as they looked at it and tried to read what it said, but they couldn't because it was written in English. I flew behind them as they took it to their nearby school so one of their teachers who knew English could read it. She read: *"For God so loved the world that He gave His only begotten Son that whoever believed in Him should not perish but would have eternal life." John 3:16.* They asked the teacher what book this was written in, and who was John, and who was the Him it was talking about? The teacher went into her classroom, got her Bible, went back outside where they were and showed them the answer of how to have the eternal life that the verse talked about.

Chapter 26
Christmas 1952

I have so many memories occurring surrounding this day and one I especially remember happened in 1954, when I was twelve-years-old.

My immediate family lived in Elberton, Georgia. Our home was on a busy street where cars and the inevitable granite trucks passed on a regular basis.

One of the natural happenings in this season was when my family went to see Nona, my paternal grandmother. We always called it 'going to the country' for she lived in the rural community of Palmetto in Oglethorpe County and there was not a lot of traffic on that dirt road.

Her name was Verona but all the adults in that area called her Miss Rona. After her first grandchild was born, that granddaughter kept hearing Miss Rona, which she couldn't pronounce, so she just said Nona. And that's the name by which she was called by her other twelve grandchildren.

I said we always went to Nona's house. It never occurred to me that we were going to the home of daddy's sister, husband and son and that Nona lived in their home. Nona's husband had died when the last of her seven children was only four years old. All her life she lived in rented houses and worked the fields to support her family. There was no such thing as Social Security then and anyway, she had never worked a public job to receive a paycheck to qualify.

In the summer of that year that family, along with Nona, had moved to Enterprise, Georgia, which was about five miles up the road.

When we got there on the Saturday before Christmas all the family had gathered, from Rayle, Elberton, Washington and Warner Robins. There was a huge decorated cedar tree in the living room and there were presents for every grandchild under it each stating that it was from Nona. We couldn't wait to open them. It never occurred to me that Nona could not have purchased twelve presents. I realized many years later that the presents had to have been supplied by our own parents.

But, we had to EAT before we could open presents! All the mamas had brought dishes to go with the food Nona and my aunt provided. It wasn't always turkey and dressing, or ham, for all those uncles were hunters and we had rabbit, squirrel, bird and maybe someone had even brought a meatloaf.

Dessert was always so special because it was homemade fruitcake, coconut cake, Lane cake or chocolate pie which had been cooked on the wood stove. We also had ambrosia made of fresh oranges, fresh coconut, grapes, and pecans with some raisins out of a box thrown in. It was so-o-o good! Then we children had to wait for our mothers to clean off the table and wash dishes before we could open presents!

Finally, we sat on the floor near the tree and one uncle called the name designated on each gift. That day mine was something I had already asked Santa Claus for - a pair of white fuzzy balls, attached to black velvet strands that you wore around your neck. I was so thrilled, now I could look like a teen-ager when I wore them to school!

Have You Found Christmas?

Have you been looking
        around and around
For the source of the joy
        that is all over town?
Have you looked in the stores
        and under the trees,
Or in the decorations
        out for all to see?
I looked and I looked
        but could not find
The source of that special joy
        in these things of our time.
Then I came upon a manger scene
        and suddenly realized,
I'd been looking in the wrong places
        for I'd been looking with my eyes.
I opened my Bible
        to Luke's second chapter
And found in his book
        the joy I was after.
It has to be in the heart
        this special joy of Christmas
It is the gift of God,
        His own Son He sent us.

Chapter 28
Hummingbirds

For the past ten plus years I have thoroughly enjoyed watching hummingbirds.

We have a covered deck at the rear of our house and I have a hummingbird feeder hanging from its rafters. I have had to refill it every two or three days the summer of 2017. At first there were only two hummingbirds, but they were later joined by a third. Hummingbirds weigh less than ½ ounce each, even though they have over 1,000 feathers. I read a book that said hummingbirds must consume ½ its weight each day. Flying as fast as they do, 30 miles per hour, and fluttering their wings 100+ times per second, must call for a lot of food. It has been such fun to watch their antics around the feeder.

One morning as I was sitting on the deck eating my breakfast cereal, one flew to the feeder which was about 10 feet away from me and began feeding. I know to be still or they will fly away but I must have moved in some way that morning for the bird backed away from the feeder, flew towards me a few feet, then flew closer, stopping two feet in front of my face. As he stopped, of course still flying, he looked at me as if to say "What are you doing in my territory?" He then flew into a nearby Dogwood Tree.

A second hummingbird flew to the feeder, but the first one flew in and chased him away before he ever got a taste! They chased one another around the feeder, out into the yard and back again. One time the two flew near each other and up to the roof rafters. They swirled, swirled, swirled around each other until they hit the floor. They weren't hurt because they then flew out into the yard.

As my kitchen window looks out onto the deck, I spent an enjoyable morning watching their antics. Later the third hummingbird came and there was all out war! All the time I watched I never saw any one of them able to light long enough to feed.

Obviously they did eat for when the feeder became almost empty I heated water and sugar and refilled it. But now it has been three days since I filled it and the feeder is still almost full. By that I assume they have migrated. Wonder how far they fly to spend the winter in a warmer climate?

Chapter 29
Little Red Wagon... What's in Yours?

When my granddaughter got married the Flower Girl walked down the center aisle dropping rose petals. She then turned and dropped rose petals as she returned UP the aisle! In the vestibule she was handed the tongue of a little red wagon in which two 18-month-old Ring Bearers, nephews of the bridal couple, sat. She then pulled the wagon to the front. Everyone was watching. "Isn't that cute," "Isn't that sweet," were the comments everyone was thinking. Let me end by saying that the Best Man then took the wagon tongue, pulled it to the side and the boys were retrieved by babysitters

Do you have a red wagon? Yes, everybody does. It may not be a physical wagon but our concerns, our fascinations, our thoughts are the make-up of the wagon that we pull behind us each day. What's in the wagon differs with each person.

How do you determine what the make-up of your wagon should be?

Let's look at some "worldly" things that should be included.

For your spouse—Verbal, or physical love is a given. But what about small everyday items like a frantic morning when everyone has to be at work/school/baby sitter by a certain time? Who can't help pour cereal out of a box, help a child pull his shirt over his head, make sure each one has the correct school books/lunch money, load the car with diaper bag, make sure car seat is in place, start car and have heater on in cool weather or air conditioner in summer, make sure that sweater or jacket is available, that wife put on her earrings, that husband got his cap or jacket...?

For a friend–to always have a smile, find out special needs of the day/week and do what you can to enable that need to be met. Sometime "call me if you need me" doesn't work so just DO whatever you see is needed.

For one who is sick—Carry to the doctor, pickup prescription, provide a meal/prepare a bowl of soup, see that their kids get to dance/piano/ball practice. After a surgery go to their home and sweep/mop, wash dishes, go to grocers, prepare/serve a meal.

For the elderly—Cut grass, rake leaves, pick up sticks/trash, transport to...

A new mother—Do anything needed to help out, even baby-sit so she can take a nap.

Now, what about some spiritual things that should be included. Everyone knows The Golden Rule-"Do unto others as you would have them do unto you," and most of us attempt to abide by it.

Romans 13:3 tells us to "do what is good." What is good? Everybody has an opinion and what's good for one is not good for another.

Is church attendance good? "Do not forsake the assembling of yourselves together," the Bible says. But if you attended worship that morning, do you now have the rest of the day free to fill as you want? Will you sit in a recliner and enjoy a ball game, cut the grass you didn't get to Saturday, go shopping and maybe see a movie?

Exodus 20:8 tells us to keep the Sabbath day holy. What does holy mean? Do you have to be holy as you think a Saint is? That is almost the meaning of holy for it means to be set aside. To be classified as a Saint a person has to have set themselves aside for some particular task that they carried out on a daily basis. One of the most recent persons made a Saint by the Catholic Church is Mother Teresa. She was canonized for her life spent in any type of service to the ill or destitute for which she saw a need. She set aside her personal wants to take care of the needs of others.

Being set aside as God wants you to be involves following His many teachings. It means spending time in His Word, the Bible, so that you will know His directions when you come upon a situation in which you wish to, or should, be involved. It means NOT taking actions that would show others that you are not following His Word.

The granddaughter I first mentioned was married more than two years ago and she recently had a baby. One of the gifts she received at a baby shower was a little red wagon filled with diapers of all sizes. I'm sure those diapers will be used and that wagon will be put to good use as a play toy when her little boy is a few years older. That is for which a physical little red wagon is made. For what purpose are you using yours?

Epilogue

This has been a joy to spend quality time, after retirement, in doing something I thoroughly enjoy. I began attending Bowers House Writers Guild in 2017 and that caused the inspiration to write the articles at close of the book, which have not been previously printed. Thanks to the Guild Director, Charles Prier, for his direction into the area of writing skill.